LIFECHANGES

WITH THE ENERGY OF THE CHAKRAS

By
Ambika Wauters

THE CROSSING PRESS
FREEDOM, CALIFORNIA

Copyright © 1999 by Ambika Wauters
Cover design by Tara M. Phillips
Interior design by Karen Narita
Printed in the USA

For information on bulk purchases or group discounts for this and other Crossing Press titles, please contact our Special Sales Manager at 800-777-1048. Visit our web site: www.crossingpress.com

Library of Congress Cataloging-in-Publication Data

Wauters, Ambika.
    Life changes : with the energy of the chakras / by Ambika Waters.
       p. cm.
    ISBN 1-58091-020-3 (pbk.)
    1. Chakras--Miscellanea. 2. Spiritual life--Miscellanea. I. Title.
BF1442.C53W42   1999
131--dc21   99-36231
                                           CIP

Contents

Acknowledgments

My sincere thanks to Dr. and Mrs. Ben Nobel for the wonderful space in which this book was written. Mill Cottage in the Lake District of England has been a haven for my spirit and creativity. The gardens and the views from the conservatory are indelibly painted in my mind's eye.

To Olevea Dewhurst-Maddox who, with grace and humor, saw me through the most powerful initiation I have experienced. She helped me see the bigger picture and bring some sense to my fears, hurt, and pain. With a skilled and caring heart she helped me find my voice.

Love to Mary Jardine, a dear friend, who always encouraged and trusted that I would do the best I could. We have been friends for lifetimes, transcending cultures, and sharing as women the insights and learnings of this New Age.

To my friend Patricia Brown who, after all these years, is still a fun companion and soul friend.

To Wendy Davis, soul sister and friend, it is so warming to know that she has touched my life with her intelligence and love for so many years.

To my aunt and uncle, Loris and Ben Cohen, and my cousins David, Paula, and Tani, for adopting me into their home and their hearts.

To Elaine Gill, who opened a door for my creativity to flow with words of encouragement and wisdom. I am so glad to be a part of The Crossing Press family.

Thank you all for having been a part of the big changes that have affected my life in such profound and positive ways. I would like this book to be a tribute to who you are.

In addition, I dedicate this book to the memory of my grandmother, a true source of unconditional love, who gave me the courage to go explore life to its depth and fullness. She remains a source of beauty, inspiration, and courage to face life's challenges.

Introduction

Disease has been described as the inability of the organism to adapt to change. If we are unable to trust in life sufficiently to see us through changes in the best possible way, we will falter in our efforts to succeed and find that we are on a downward spiral of negativity. Finding wholesome ways to manage and understand change offers us a unique opportunity for growth and healing.

When we face up to the reality of change we learn to accept its challenges with grace and renewed grit. Whining about being victimized, maligning others, and blaming them as the source of our problems not only make us sound petty and mean, it also enforces old patterns of behavior, and we will project our negativity onto others rather than taking responsibility for ourselves. This will not serve either our psychological growth or our spiritual development. Instead, it will keep us fixed in patterns of response that limit our happiness, pleasure, and joy.

By understanding how we respond to change and the effect it has on our energy system, we can alter these old patterns of response and gain insight into our nature. By coming to accept the inevitability of change, we will be released from the past, able to find new, healthy options for our lives. Change opens doors so we can see opportunities for creativity and health. At this point we understand that it is offering us a challenge to become a better person.

Change teaches us about the mystery of life and our part in its unfolding. As our potential is systematically transformed into a kinetic force that enhances our life force and takes us to higher ground, we become more of who we are. As I look back on my life over the past ten years, I can see that my emotional issues around change have corresponded to the development of my energy centers. They helped to open up my higher centers of perception. I now measure my life changes by the levels of energy, vitality, and empowerment I have, not by what has happened externally. I value the insights about who I am at every level that change reveals.

Our chakras are subtle organs that act as conductors for change. When we suppress our emotions and have not dealt with our negativity, the chakras become congested. At that point our energy level goes down, and we block the natural flow of life, resulting in stagnation, disease, chronic problems, and premature aging.

Change and how we handle it reflect our levels of adaptability, maturity, and understanding of reality. Change affects us on all levels. It influences our health, our emotional well-being, mental clarity, and physical vitality. How we respond to change is a reflection of our old patterns of behavior, our present state of awareness, and our belief in ourselves.

We have control of our lives to the degree that we can be detached witnesses looking at the way we behave in the midst of change. If we perpetually blame others and look outside ourselves for answers, we lose the golden thread of self-awareness that change gives us and forget the underlying purpose of change. These big transitions are meant to bring us closer to the light within ourselves, to the depths of our understanding, and to the place where healing can occur. There are no changes, no matter how severe or grotesque, which are not meant to strengthen us, enhance our love for ourselves, and hopefully open our hearts to the inner light which some call the Christos, the Buddha, or the inner temple. In the realm of possibilities, change is our way of shifting to new insights and awareness about our true nature.

We can use the chakras as a framework for monitoring change. We can find out where our energy is blocked and needs transformation. When we do this, we are able to heal what is dysfunctional in our behavior. This is empowering. It gives us a handle to deal with life. As Joseph Murphy, a mentor of mine, once said, "It is not the gale, but the set of your sail which determines the way you go." It is our attitude, the way we relate to change, that will ultimately affect the outcome of the situation.

The first book I wrote on the chakras, Healing with the Energy of the Chakras, outlined the major chakras of the Human Energy System. As I examined the nature of each chakra, its emotional issues, and its different aspects, I explained how to heal its congested energy. The book was designed as a self-help guide to working with subtle energy. It is the basis for the workshop I offer.

The second book, The Chakras and Their Archetypes, explored the archetypes of empowerment, vitality, and responsibility as they relate to the chakras. It shows how we can transform our negative attitudes about ourselves and our lives. This book came out of my experience of living in a foreign country and studying hard training as a homeopath, while trying to maintain a tempestuous and difficult relationship. The book is the result of understanding how we become empowered and gain greater levels of energy as we take more and more responsibility for ourselves.

As I faced massive changes in my life, I found myself having to rewrite that book over and over again. I had just turned fifty, had recently lost a good friend in a shockingly sudden way, had just completed an arduous seven year training, and had ended a three year relationship. Change was all I could see in my life. I kept falling into the Victim archetype and with every rewrite needed to examine my attitudes and behavior. I was surprised to find that I had written my own self-help manual. I used that manual to put me onto higher ground psychologically and spiritually. It was an eventful time in my life.

One of the big lessons I learned from this period was that it didn't matter what I did or where I lived—the issues I needed to confront were not going to go away. When I asked my friend Sue Bell what she thought about my moving back to the States, she told me it didn't matter where I lived. She was right. My life would continue to unfold and the issues that needed sorting out were going to continue to stare me in the face until I addressed them.

This is how I had a firsthand experience about my own archetypes. The best choice for me was to remain in Britain and go on working both as a homeopath and facilitator for the chakra workshops I had created. During this time I put together a long-term program for women who wanted to develop their awareness of energy and simultaneously grow emotionally and spiritually. Those two endeavors, I now realize, taught me more about myself and the nature of life change than anything I had ever undertaken. They became the vehicles for me to grow and face my limitations as well as my gifts. Understanding the nature of change gave me a deeper awareness about what is permanent and stable within us as well as what brings peace to our hearts and minds, even during tumultuous times.

This book is about life changes and energy. It comes out of my awareness and insights during that grounding and healing period of my life. It was an intense period of growth which tried me, toughened me up, and ultimately gave me the confidence that I could manage my life no matter what. As I became more stable in my work and gained confidence in my ability to help people process their heavy physical and emotional burdens, my life became richer and deeper. I have grown and come to respect how healing happens to us with incremental shifts in perception.

I have recently completed eighteen months of chakra training and eight years of practice as a Classical Homeopath. I have seen how people change as they let go of their negativity and allow their lives to unfold in a healthy way. They may have a difficult and painful time, but ultimately they recognize that life change provided a unique opportunity to find their true selves and fortify their spirit.

People's ability to assimilate their experiences and synthesize wisdom is what turns them into compassionate, spiritual beings. This differentiates them from those who remain fixed, negative, and unhappy, who constantly blame others for how bad their lives are. It has been a privilege to meet so many remarkable people in my practice and in the training who have been willing to make appropriate changes in their lives. They have grown in stature and character, taken fuller responsibility for their lives, and shifted layers of negativity which were draining their life forces. Their healthy attitudes have made them strong. I salute those who have come to grips with their lives and brought healing to themselves and to others.

I have witnessed many changes in people and seen how they have experienced greater choice, more vitality, and greater responsibility, as well as enjoying immense happiness and joy. The result of such hard work is that we are better able to experience life, find healthy and wholesome solutions to our problems, and enjoy greater levels of self-acceptance. This is what peace and freedom are about.

I am on the brink of another major life change. I am returning to America after being away for a full Saturn cycle of twenty-eight years that began when I was twenty-six years old and my mother passed away. In these twenty-eight years I traveled extensively in Spain, Belgium, Africa, and Britain. I have now come to the age my mother was when she died. I now feel ready to accept my gifts of creativity and healing which have grown during this cycle. It has been a time of accepting and recognizing who I am.

I suspect that Saturn, known as the reaper because it forces us to ground our spirit and realize our gifts, helps us to be absolutely clear about who we are and what our purpose is in life. When we know this, change becomes more than an event we have to deal with. It isn't a random thing, taking our breath away, leaving us dismayed. Rather, it offers us the next step, the next challenge, the next purifier of our spirit.

There is an old Chinese saying that says great gifts ripen late. Though I knew very much the same things at twenty-eight that I know now, it has taken me this long to strengthen my inner Self, develop my character, learn to stand on my own two feet, support myself, and deal with life. Having any kind of talent also means developing the protective skills necessary to allow it to flourish.

Learning to say no when something did not feel right, insisting that something be looked at again and reconsidered, protesting when I felt that I was being manipulated or taken advantage of, learning to walk away when something was going to pull me in and drain me—these steps created a shield for the soft, absorbent, very sensitive interior that was often fragile, and struggled with relationships. I learned to honor myself, acknowledge that my process was unique and at times out of sync with my friends and work obligations, and give myself pats on the back for bravery and courage when I did something that required more guts than I thought I had.

Honoring our deep inner nature is how we identify that unchanging bedrock of our being, that part of us which doesn't change or alter, no matter what happens or what we do. This is the part that is a constant, stable force, which will not let us be swept away by the waves of change or betray us when we are less than perfect. This is the part of us that never changes, that has always been and will always be without question. It is eternal, non-negotiable, and always on our side. It defies values or ideas that go in and out of fashion, and it never alters. It is the Self, non-mutable, all-knowing, and all-caring. Life change puts us in touch with it. It is what I call the Self or Christos.

Change doesn't frighten me as it used to. I now accept it and welcome it as part of the ongoing process to which I am committed. I have reconciled myself to its inevitability and to what is permanent with me as well. Whatever the life change may be, that part that is permanently, shining within me, will always be there lighting the way forward through endless dimensions of reality. Life has taught me we can't afford to resist its mystery or hide our gifts. Coming into the light and living comfortably with who we really are, accepting our gifts as well as our limitations, is how we find balance and achieve a sense of wholeness.

The more I realize the nature of cycles, large and small, which define our life patterns, the more I see that there are optimal moments in which change occurs. Whenever I ask people when major events like divorce, separation, and loss happened to them, invariably it generally coincided with a major astrological cycle such as a Saturn or a Uranus return. It is therefore sometimes useful to warn people they are about to go on a roller coaster ride for a time. This awareness not only prepares them for change, it also may open new dimensions to their lives that will ultimately help them grow and develop.

Change has one purpose and that is to help us discover ourselves. What happens to us is not as important as how we handle what happens. We can be martyrs and victims, begrudging life its changes, or we can be warriors, lovers, and gurus learning to flow with the forces that direct our lives. The people I admire the most are those spiritual warriors who accept change and have profited immensely from change.

When I look back on what I have experienced, struggled with, and wept over I realize that all of it was meant to take me to higher ground. Sometimes I need to remember to be thankful for that magnificent creator within me that materialized these wonderful opportunities for growth and development. The mystery of the inner Self which directs these events is beyond the scope of any writer, filmmaker, or playwright to imagine. At best, they try to imitate the wonder and magnificence of life.

Most of the changes that happen in our lives are the inevitable consequence of our consciousness and our need to grow and experience life more fully. As we choose to let go and allow the inner Self to guide us during times of change, we find that we are able to jump hurdles that previously seemed insurmountable. Finding the resiliency to face challenges continually is what keeps us youthful and adventurous. When we let go of stale patterns of identification and the "shoulds" which make us resist change, we have the opportunity to grow and deepen our relationship with life. In doing so, our perceptions become more finely tuned, our humor deepens, our vitality strengthens, and life becomes infinitely more joyful.

It is important to remember that the price of our consciousness has been paid for by the steps to freedom our ancestors and parents were willing to take. We must acknowledge also the struggles of lifetimes past which expanded our inner knowing and strengthened our being. Our present consciousness is built on foundations of love that have brought us through ordeals and struggles with ourselves to a place of self-respect and self-worth where we are able to honor our inner life and value the Source within. It helps us to remember that life is, at its core, good, loving, and kind.

I hope that you will enjoy this book. It will help you to accept the inevitability of change as part of your life and to choose your path consciously and confidently. You will have to accept the challenges that change brings. It is a time to learn about who you are. It will teach you how to enjoy precious moments of peace, love, and friendship when they come to you. It will show you how to grasp the humor of a situation over which you have absolutely no control and to laugh till your sides ache. It will help you manage your time and energy so that change works for you, not against you. It can help you endure the long hauls required to bring your dreams and creative projects to fruition.

When you accept the truth of change you will be better able to regenerate your spirit when your well is empty and to find room in your heart to ask for help when you need it. Change teaches you to be more accepting of yourself, your capacities, and your gifts. When you reach this stage, you can make conscious decisions about your future. Then change will become just part of your life, a natural consequence of your inner development.

This isn't a book with recipes. It will give you the best of my insight about how to look at change, and it will provide you with ways in which you can choose wholesome options that will result in your healing. The methods I offer here have helped me through the hard events in my life—death, divorce, financial uncertainty, aging, retraining, and immigration. Through these crises I eventually made the conscious choice to grow up and take responsibility for love, work, and friendship in my life. I hope you find this book useful for getting through the corridors of life changes. I wish you the best of luck and real happiness.

Life Changes and Energy

"Change is the root of life."
—An old Hebrew maxim

When we accept change as an integral part of life, we become attuned to the flow of universal intelligence that resonates within us as the life force, orchestrating the changes we must undergo to open our hearts and purify our spirits. Yet, most of us are not ready or willing to follow the path that life lays out for us. Instead, we find ourselves resisting that path, and by doing so we become ill and afraid.

How people adapt to change molds their character and creates the context in which wisdom, growth, and consciousness develop and thrive. As part of the law of progression, change will eventually enable us to teach others how they too can adapt to change. This is called the path of the Elders. The more we are able to accept the inevitability of change, the less we will suffer from its effects, and eventually we will reach a point where we consciously direct the changes we wish to make. When this happens we become empowered.

Most people are afraid to let go of their fixed ideas, and as a consequence change becomes something dreaded and resisted. Most people fear the loss of their personal identifications: social position, job status, wealth or the lack of it, age, sexuality and allure, parental status and marital status. They fear that they will appear smaller than the image they wish to project—someone who is important or in control. They fail to recognize themselves in the context of the world they inhabit. If your identity, who you think you are, is linked with external identifications, change becomes something dreaded.

Our lives will always be subject to change, and this can ultimately bring us to the awareness of our inner being, that eternal part of us known as the Christos which is eternal, never to be born, never to die. Without change we have no way of finding out who we really are and what is permanent within us.

If we are love, peace, and truth and this is eternal, why do we constantly have to make changes in order to keep up? We obviously need a grasp of both external and internal realities. If we are immersed in the exterior world (the reality of aging, job loss, personal power, and financial success), it can consume a great deal of our time and energy. If we are focused inwardly on spirit, we lose the opportunities for personal growth that come from ego development and meeting life's challenges. Without meeting the demands of a worldly life, we remain immature, unable to fend for ourselves, and unable to develop the personal wisdom that maturity and life experience bring us.

Fortunately, both the inner approach and the outer reality can merge to form a developed spirit and a strong, resilient ego. We can learn to cope with change in the outer world and at the same time anchor our identity in our spirit. This is the middle way, the way of the Spiritual Warrior.

When changes come as they surely must, people who are too strongly attached to their external tags of identification will lack the resiliency and resources to manage. When we feel unloved, rejected, or not good enough, we find ourselves living out the archetype of the Victim. Some people are so overwhelmed by a life change, their minds freeze and their bodies become paralyzed. Sometimes these reactions appear as anxiety attacks that result in acute physical and emotional states. Eventually the organism shuts down, and disease results. Seldom do we associate what happens with the person's resistance to change. When such illness occurs, the vital life force is telling us that our attitude toward life needs to be addressed and that our inner Self is not in harmony with the external realities. We are inevitably forced to learn how to manage change.

In homeopathy, we define disease as the organism's inability to adapt to change. For example, when a person goes out into the cold without sufficient clothing and is chilled, his temperature drops, and to compensate for the cold his body produces a fever, resulting in aches and pains. The body always tries to maintain balance.

Germs and viruses are always with us. They will attack an organism when it's immune system is weakened by its inability to adapt to change. The result can be emotional as well as physical stress. When a person holds on to grief, anger, and resentment, the organism may be threatened in the same way and develop an illness that may be fatal.

Sometimes people's need to be right is so great it will overwhelm their desire to be healthy. One of the cancer patients I treated said on her deathbed she wished she had let go of her resentment years ago. She had been so attached to pitying herself and blaming her former husband, she had no energy left over to fight her illness. Whenever we see chronic disease patterns, we always ask when the condition began because it will inevitably coincide with an emotional issue which was not resolved. It almost always came at a difficult time when they were caught in the whirlwind of change and could not adapt. Tests have shown that if people ignore their feelings, within two years after a major life change they become ill.

Consciousness helps us to forgive ourselves when we aren't as perfect as we would like to be. It can take years after an event to understand fully what it really meant. Often our final understanding will be quite different from the time when we were overwhelmed with our initial emotions. Being slow to judge and quick to accept will help us get through such difficult times with a minimum of distress. If there is an issue which needs to be brought to light, our Higher Self will always present it to us in the form of a situation which asks us to respect our inner process as a time for change. This is the time we are most likely to learn the universal truths of life.

The Higher Self not only has a great sense of humor—its timing is also impeccable. We get the lessons we need at the precise time we are ready for them. This makes change the natural fomenter of growth and development, the medium in which we mature and garner wisdom. If we can let go of the status quo, we have a real opportunity to mature into wise and capable people.

When we are ready to handle self-sufficiency, the Higher Self will throw us into deep water. When it is time to surrender to love, that same positive and creative force within us will bring someone into our lives who will teach us to open our hearts and learn the power of love. When we are ready to manage greater levels of responsibility, events will happen which will engage our talent and abilities. Life gives us all the chance we need in order to grow. We don't have to look for change; it is usually waiting for us. Its purpose is to help us let go of our resistance and embrace our lives.

Having the resources to handle change is important; otherwise people become so depleted and drained that the way back to health and vitality can be cut off. Most people do not realize how much energy it takes to be able to manage change effectively. They delude themselves that they do not need assistance, support, and time to assimilate or to rest from the intensity of their experience. When we are struggling, we can ask for help from a friend or pray. When we tap into the realm of spirit, we quickly learn that we are not alone and, indeed, have never been alone. The guidance of higher beings is always available to us. We need only ask. There is a wonderful story told in Ireland of a man walking in the sand by the sea looking back on his life when he notices two sets of footprints which were there from the time of his birth to the present. One set belongs to him, the other belongs to his guardian angel. As he looks back on the tracks he sees that at certain points of difficulty there was only one set of prints. He comments on this, and his angel responds that those were the times he carried the man on his back when he wasn't able to walk on his own.

Often when people are ill they do not have the physical or the spiritual resources to handle major change by themselves. They are using their resources simply to stay alive. Help can be given in many ways: time, rest, good food, friends, support groups, and money. Even interesting work can be therapeutic when a person is making a major change. Sometimes just having enough money, friends, courage, or spiritual belief can get a person through a bad time. Or just knowing what is important helps make those shifts easier. Trusting you will get your needs met one way or another is part of trusting the inner process of life to unfold as it should.

We have all seen people in the flux of change who did not have the right resources. They had little confidence, were fearful, worried, or attached to the past. If change is waiting to happen, what do you really need to take the next step? How are you going to get what you need?

Sometimes we think if we had more money or better friends the next step would be easy, when in fact the next step may simply be knowing that you have everything you need to go forward, that what you want can be attained simply with patience and clarity of mind.

I often wonder what would happen if we were able to give people what they think they need. Many people need to struggle. They stage a continuous saga of chaos—drama gives their lives meaning. They cannot accept ease, happiness, or peace, unless it is hard won. Take the drama away and they are left in a psychological vacuum, starved for spiritual food. Eventually the strain of this dysfunction becomes evident, usually taking the form of sickness.

The body thrives and flourishes on peace and happiness, and deteriorates under prolonged pressure. Tension creates a weakened immune system and an inability to adapt to change. We need to detach ourselves from our situations from time to time in order to see what we are doing to our precious life force. The first step is to see what we don't want, and then imagine what we do want.

One full moon some Native American women met for their monthly sweat lodge where they exchanged gossip and stories. One evening a middle-aged squaw confided that her husband beat her, her son took drugs, and life was terrible. Her sisters gave her sympathy as well as sound advice, telling her not to take her husband's abuse, but to report it to the elders. She agreed with their counsel. At the next moon gathering she repeated that her husband beat her, her son took drugs, and life was terrible. They asked if she had really understood their advice. She said she did. They remained silent. At the third full moon she repeated once more that her husband beat her, her son took drugs, and life was terrible, whereupon the women got up from the sweat circle and left her there alone. She got the message. When you complain repeatedly, but do not change your life, the world will give you a strong message that it is time to do something.

We need to know that we are worthy and can call upon our inner resources to make change a positive reality. It helps when we are happy and find delight in abundance, love, and joy. Unfortunately, most people have a strong root memory of hardship that causes them to repeat the old pattern of making changes difficult. I have seen patients who became better with treatment and then suddenly developed another problem that prevented them from doing something creative with their lives. They have no real faith in themselves or their ability to create a good life. Health goes hand in hand with independence of spirit and the ability to make a meaningful life with satisfying work and loving relationships.

What is change? How can we make it a tool for growth in our lives? Learning to manage time, energy, and personal resources is a skill that can help us through life changes. How much time does it take for us to learn that anything that leaves us tired and drained does not serve us? If we have an underlying belief in drudgery as a necessary part of life, we will perpetuate it for eternity, rather than change how we view it as a part of our life.

When we dislike our jobs, we will be drained of energy, indicating that there is a leak somewhere in our system. By listening to our bodies and observing our patterns of hardship and denial, we can discover what we need to work on. We can begin by asking ourselves if our current job is good for us. Do we feel that we have the right to be happy? If the answer is yes, we need to make positive changes. If the answer is no, we need to do some soul-searching.

We can look at the Root Chakra to see whether our beliefs enhance our life or not. This is the center where we embrace or deny life changes. It is worth examining our underlying beliefs about appropriate work, a good life, survival, and duty. Negative attitudes often reflect an underlying suspicion about sexuality, pleasure, abundance, and happiness. This negativity is an indication that we feel we have to suffer, that no happiness is possible for us. It is an indication that the Sacral Charka is blocked. Do we have some inner work to do to clear the chakra and remove the negativity? By failing to move forward in life, we diminish the energy in the Solar Plexus. We need to build a healthy ego so that we will be able to negotiate in our lives.

In my homeopathic practice people come to see me because at some level they are stuck, unable to make the shifts necessary to move forward in life. Though their plight might be masked by an illness, their lives are on hold. They could use their illness as a way to grow or as a way to stay stuck. We all have the choice about how we want to progress through life—as victims or as empowered human beings.

A friend of mine recently decided that she wanted to make a major move to a new country and needed a job that matched her skills. After nine months of failing to find what she wanted she awoke one morning and said to herself, "I can make this work." That very day she found the job that was right for her and her life moved ahead. It was a small but significant shift in her perception about herself, her sense of worth, and her level of confidence. We all have had similar experiences when the shift takes only a second.

Creativity forms a context in which confidence and self-empowerment can flourish. When sick people begin to heal, they find they can use their newfound energy for creative pursuits which in turn can open a channel for more healing. Doing something creative in which you take pride can make a big difference in your view of yourself. In general, people become energized in their interchanges with people and by tackling difficult tasks. Sometimes people have a genetic weakness that can be triggered by stress. They appear to have little control over such a predisposed condition, but doing something creative can free up the life force to release stress and help them feel better about themselves. A change of attitude usually goes hand in hand with taking a risk and doing something new you avoided before.

The body/mind/spirit has its strengths and weaknesses when it reacts to stress. In homeopathy, we call this compensation, the way the vital force protects a person under stress. Even illness can help when the body tries to adjust to changing conditions. I recently heard a story which is a good example of this. An old dog was becoming lame and slowed down appreciably. His lameness protected him from accidents. His owner gave him herbs and he got better, but was killed because he couldn't respond quickly enough to get across the road in time.

Sometimes accepting the inevitability of change is wisdom. When we interfere, we often create another set of problems that need to be solved.

Learning to read the body as a metaphor for resistance or openness is helpful in understanding ourselves. Attitudes of rigidity, fear, and weakness are all emotional holding patterns locked into the musculature. Predisposition to strain, inflammation, and congestion are also symptoms. A person who has trouble walking may need to slow down mentally long enough to see what he is running from. A person whose arthritis gets worse when he suppresses his anger must learn to be comfortable with his feelings. Rigidity implies early suppression of feelings; fear is evident in tight shoulders, neck, and scalp muscles.

What we call the vital force in homeopathy is built into our subconscious mind. We need to learn how to tap into it consciously to recreate higher levels of well-being, abundance, and healing. We have to put in new programs for the subconscious mind in order to activate expanded dimensions of healing and wholeness that correspond to empowered levels of self-image and self-worth.

When we affirm who we are and give ourselves permission to have the things we want in life, we free up energy that has been tied up maintaining old patterns of resistance. This released energy gives us the vitality we need for new creative outlets. One of the ways we can reprogram ourselves is to inform our inner Child to let go of past wounds. To trust life and the body's responses will result in a surge of renewed vigor and energy. Symptoms clear up quickly when we free up emotional energy which is being suppressed or somatized in physical distress.

The physical body is a mirror of the mind. People who understand this can handle change in positive ways. They can manage physical symptoms without fear, and as they accept the challenges life presents, they experience new degrees of insight. What transpires is a revolving spiral of success, health, and happiness that intensifies as they take more responsibility for their well-being.

In a chakra training program I was able to monitor emotional, mental, and physical changes in myself and in the ten women who completed the training. We all had particular strengths and weaknesses that were related to our profession as caretakers. There is a pathology that corresponds to all professions. Our pathology could be traced back to our need to be cared for early in childhood. Through projection, we translated our need to be taken care of to our need to take care of others. Our inner changes dealt mainly with owning our power and developing healthy egos. Whenever one of us had success in the world we celebrated it unanimously. Most of the women managed to keep their egos in balance as they went through life changes, and they achieved a higher degree of empowerment during the training. However, there were a few women who were unwilling to work through their blocks. They remained stuck in old patterns of negative projection and reverted to acts of hostility and sabotage. In any training some people do well while others clearly need more time.

This work gave me an opportunity to grow as a person and as a teacher, and also gave me the opportunity to observe how inner and outer changes affected energy. Finding the balance between aggression and receptivity, openness and protection, is serious work. It is hard for many people to find the strong, resilient sense of Self that is necessary for good relationships, financial security, and creativity. Such a strong sense of Self will help people so that they can stop being victims. It tells them they deserve the good things in life.

Most people who work with energy will tell you that as their patients begin to heal, they look more attractive and are more at ease. They are closer to their feelings, can cry with pain, shout with anger, and express themselves openly. When positive changes happen, people develop the confidence to look their best. Weight shifts, skin glows, posture becomes more erect. People become transformed and their creativity begins to soar. New and exciting things begin to happen. This is what health is.

Often changes occurred which were very impressive. I could see the visible evidence of weight loss, new haircuts, new physical vitality, and new, appropriate self-images, all of which reflected a deep, inner knowing. I saw faces open, eyes twinkle, jaws release their tension, shoulders drop, chests expand, legs strengthen, and humor and insight made evident. My own feet expanded one full shoe size during the training when my friend Judy Jones, a brilliant body therapist in Denver, Colorado, gave me three sessions. I had a deep fear of being grounded which she addressed. She released the deep tension locked in my small, immature feet for a lifetime. I had to release my fear of life and become clearer about what I wanted to do and how to implement the changes necessary to allow those things to happen.

In the training we could see transformation when we compared early with late photos taken over the eighteen month training program. This became a very important part of our group meetings. We could experience the shifts in consciousness as we let go of dysfunctional attitudes, released excess psychological baggage, and began to take more responsibility for ourselves. The whole group's energy became more refined, more attuned, gentler.

When we looked back through our journals we saw the incremental shifts in consciousness that happened when we changed our perception of ourselves. This always brought us to new levels of growth, awareness, and a deeper bonding between us. The women shared their insights and developed real feelings of friendship and sisterhood. They also developed into good teachers.

What is resistance? It is holding on to the past, that can manifest as cynicism, criticism, stubbornness, complaints, and confusion. Such negativity will prevent us from perceiving the good in the moment. It absorbs vital life energy. In the body, resistance manifests as headaches, migraines, chest infections, stomach upsets, constipation, even athlete's foot. It can be seen in the shape of the jaw, the jut of the chin, and the distant gaze in the eye.

The questionnaire at the end of each chapter was designed during this training. It was helpful for each participant. It will help you look at the issues in your life that may need change and help you see where you are resistant. It will help you make conscious choices when you are ready to let go of old, worn-out ideas. Resistance stops life from flowing. It creates reservoirs of energy that stagnate, even though our energy system longs for outlets of expression. Even if the risks are high and you are vulnerable, you will never know what you are capable of unless you share yourself with the world.

Use the tools in this book as a guide to help you through challenging situations or in the long periods when you need support. If you can form a healing circle with a group of committed friends, you can also reap the benefits of sharing, supporting, and bonding while undergoing change. Just looking at the things that stop you from having the life you say you want can be of real value. You may find that true healing comes from acceptance and sharing. Identifying self-imposed stumbling blocks can help you see what you put in the way of love. It's freeing to know that if you put those blocks there, you can also remove them.

This book is about the nature of change as it affects us individually. With the colossal changes occurring on our planet, personal internal changes are happening to everyone. How each person handles change helps to set the tone for global and even cosmic shifts in consciousness. It is also important to remember that in the healing process no one ever heals alone. When one person is uplifted, others always follow.

Facing the challenges that come with healthy choices requires energy and knowing how to conserve our gains and invest in our growth. When we value ourselves sufficiently to feel we are worth something, we fashion a template of positive energy through visualization, meditation, and affirmation, which then becomes a magnet in attracting wholesome life experiences to us. This acts as a model for our life and our experiences will fill that model, making it real.

This book can help liberate, conserve, and ultimately maximize your energy while you amend your perceptions, thus introducing new levels of stamina and insight into your life. Assimilating and digesting change is the same internal psychological and mental process as digesting the food we eat. Situations and people will or will not nurture us. If they don't, we may need to reflect on what sort of situations and people *will* nurture us and trust that we have everything within us to implement those needs. Some people can eat rich food while others can't. Some sick people cannot absorb minerals or other vital nutrients from the food they eat because their systems are so fragile. It is the same with life changes. Sometimes because of our fears, we cannot assimilate the goodness that comes to us, and we resist the challenges that face us. Many people are not capable of assimilating the good without reverting to old, addictive patterns of denial and therefore starve themselves of the joys and pleasures of life.

Other people hold old beliefs that make them expect the worst, and as a result they often get it. They love the drama of their negativity, and it keeps them from looking at who they are. Many people grieve because they have denied themselves goodness for so long; they still must dig in their heels resisting change. I also find that people are as afraid of positive experiences as they are of difficult ones. They simply don't know how to embrace goodness. Learning to let pleasure in and enjoy the simple things in life is important if we are going to roll with the punches that life changes bring. This is one of the real lessons of change.

Accepting change also requires spiritual, mental, and emotional grounding. If we say we want something, we need to make the internal space to receive it. We need to harvest out our negativity in order to do this. As we create the context for change in our life, it is important to expand our capacity to digest our experiences. This may mean releasing negative thoughts, freeing people by forgiving them, and letting go of past failures in order to create more room for the people and things we enjoy.

As we expand our vision of life we create a richer and broader context with which to embrace it. It's like a chalice that holds the holy water of life. We baptize ourselves with this holy water when we allow ourselves to be in our experience, feel our feelings, and tell our truths. This requires finding the time to reflect and listen to our inner spiritual guidance. It also means being able to accept our lives simply and lovingly as a gift, and being grateful for what we have made of our lives and our talents. It opens the space for new things to come.

Transforming our inner reality comes from the awareness of ourselves as part of the greater whole. The irony is that it comes only when we are ready for it—it never comes too soon or too late. Accepting life is how we emerge masterful through ups and downs. By denying change we remain fixed in a universe where the only constant is change itself. If we have a spiritual and philosophical context in which to hold change, we can view our resistance and negativity with detachment and compassion.

Resistance manifests itself whenever there is fear, denial, withdrawal, or separation. We can palpate it in the body. It feels hard, unyielding, and fixed. We experience it when hearts remain closed and there is little enthusiasm for the joyful things around us. Yet resistance is a natural and unconscious reaction to change. To free ourself from its clutches, we simply need to acknowledge it as a part of the process of growth. When we have a context for accepting change, then resistance is acceptable. Within a spiritual context we embrace our negativity. We become our own best friends and allow our feelings to be what they are.

Alternative Practices for Managing Change

The word chakra is Hindi in origin—it means wheel of light, essentially a vortex where energy from the cosmos and from the earth plane converges to form a swirling source of energy. Chakras are nonatomical centers where energy is filtered into and out of the physical body. Made of fine, etheric substance, they act as conductors of energy—from the refined energy of our spirit to the grosser energy of our physical being. There are seven main chakras in the human energy system plus twenty-one minor chakras. The acupuncture points are still smaller chakras.

One way we can transmute resistance to life is by working with the chakras for wholeness and growth. They are models for how subtle energy moves in and through our body. They also respond to our emotional patterns, belief systems, and levels of personal responsibility and empowerment. Their function is fundamental to our health, vitality, and ability to go forward in life.

We are a complete bioenergetic system living within a biosphere of energy that is fed and nourished through an interchange with other people and with nature. Our biosphere is synergistically connected to all life, visible and invisible. What happens at an energetic level will be reflected in everyone and everything around you. No one is separate from this system. A healthy ego will define its boundaries and at the same time see itself as part of the whole.

The human biosphere is known as the aura. The seven main chakras are contained within it. They hold the truth of an individual's physical, emotional, mental, and spiritual life. If there is resistance, it will manifest in the energetic system and show up in the chakra that most closely corresponds to the emotional issue at hand. For instance, if people are blocked in their personal expression they will have a congested Throat Chakra. If they are blocked in sexuality they will have a congested Sacral Chakra.

If you wish to counter your resistance at this energetic level, you must be willing to be honest with yourself. Once you know where you are blocked, you can use various techniques to open and balance that chakra. Thought transforms energy. If we think that we are worthy of goodness, love, and empowerment, we can expand the levels of energy moving through our system. But if we feel we are unworthy, we limit our energy and shrink our life force. One of the things we can do is to reprogram how we think about ourselves—it will change our energy levels. Whenever we are negative or unloving to ourselves or others, we clog the channels through which energy flows. Conversely, when we release our negativity and let our true inner light shine forth, we clear the avenues for energy to flow freely through us. This is called healing.

Affirming ourselves means being willing to look at our lives to experience our self-worth. This may take some practice, especially in situations where we are not used to being right, or even acknowledged. Loving ourselves, no matter what transpires in the events of our external life, is the way we heal our wounds. Chronic negativity can weaken our life force, thus stimulating the roots of disease. The physical, emotional, and spiritual body thrives on love and self- acceptance.

When we surrender to how we feel and what we think about ourselves, we can make choices on where we want to focus our awareness and energy. For instance, if our confidence is low, we may want to do inner work that will build our self-esteem. If we are cerebral and unconscious on a physical level, we may wish to do body work or get into a program where we can become aware of our bodies. If we realize we are immature and afraid of intimacy, we can look at our parental issues. The more negativity we hold onto, the harder each advance in consciousness will be.

People who struggle with themselves also struggle in life. Struggle with the Self can make us think that we are wrong whereas others are right, or that we are not good enough. We will never feel right in our bodies; events and people will never be quite right or satisfying. There will always be a feeling that our cup is half empty rather than half full.

Negativity can manifest in every aspect of our life. Examining how we look at ourselves and embracing the unloved parts will save us the energy we would spend in defending ourselves or feeding our self-hatred.

When we engage with stress, the Self becomes pressured to be or do something beyond its limits. The cycles and rhythms of life become disrupted, and the body/mind/spirit is pushed beyond its capacity. However, because change is necessary for growth, we know that through training the body and the mind we can both develop an expanded capacity to work and live. In this case stress may be an opportunity to grow. Whenever we train, whether it is for a stronger body or a more developed mind, we put pressure on ourselves to expand and grow. The more positive we are in our approach to this work, the greater the possibility to achieve what we want for ourselves in life.

There are even times that illness serves our conscious growth and development, not only by removing old negativity and letting in room for new, kinder thoughts, but by showing us where we can affirm ourselves. Illness can bring us an awareness of what we have been doing to ourselves and what we need in order to be healthier.

Expansion is a natural part of growth. Allowing ourselves a larger arena in which to work and play is a way of saying yes to life and yes to ourselves. Change and resistance to change form the energetic dynamic of each individual. Meeting a challenge with our best intentions in play, will show us who we are. Resisting life means narrowing its possibilities, whereas opening ourselves up will widen its possibilities, giving us a deeper and richer perspective.

There are many things you can do to help you swim through life change. They can quicken the transit through blocked emotions and congested energy. They can help conserve your vitality and support you through difficult times. Over the years I have found these tools to be most helpful for my peace of mind: meditation, prayer, affirmations, visualization, rebirthing, homeopathy, acupuncture, massage, exercise, good nutrition, rest, and support. Some of these have become part of my daily routine, others are reserved for times of exhaustion and depletion, or when I simply need time out, or when I wished to tap into a deeper, more knowing part of myself. I learned to value these tools as I would precious jewelry, good books, and dear friends. They are part of my survival kit.

Some of these things you can do on your own, others require help from friends to see you through, or professional help for special insight or support. Be willing to invest in your well-being. It will save your health and give you the energy you need to make the necessary changes. If you are stuck and can't see the horizon, or if you have been suffering too long, good professional advice can make a difference. Professionals know what they are doing and can give you the awareness to move into a new level of empowerment.

Learning to manage energy is what makes us masters of change. We can tap into our inner strength to handle the uncertainties, challenges, and chaos swirling around us. Being true to our inner beliefs about the goodness of life and the power of love, light, and healing will sustain us when we are in transition. This belief will connect us with our inner nature so that we know that everything will eventually be okay, no matter how trying the situation is. Without that inner guidance and a strong, positive belief system, we can fall into a vapid chasm of dependency.

Everyone indulges in psychic thumb-sucking from time to time, but as my good friend, clairvoyant Alexandra Anderson, used to tell me, "Do it for ten minutes, not ten hours." Things that drain life energy, such as excessive mourning, exhaustive crying, and deeply suppressed rage need to be addressed with detachment. Ask yourself if what you are doing is really good for you. If the answer is yes, allow it. If the answer is no, acknowledge that you are being self-indulgent. Tell yourself that your attitude is depleting your energy, tell yourself to get on with your life. Excessive acting out will diminish your energy, whereas being objective about your attitude can make the difference between suffering a debilitating disease or taking a few days off to regenerate. The more indulgent you are, the more it will ultimately cost you in time and resources.

There are certain flower essences, foods, and vitamins that will help you keep up your energy balanced. What works for you? Do you need meat when your energy is low? It may be important to examine your diet as well as your belief system in order to find out which foods nourish you. Meat can be medicine when you are anemic or exhausted. Ancient people have known this and given thanks to the animals that sacrificed themselves for human welfare. It is important to listen to what your body wants when you are stressed. Big changes sometimes require a lot of physical energy. Living on minimal food when you are going through change may exhaust you. The brain and the body both require appropriate food. There are good supplements and homeopathic medicines that can tonify the mind and help the body under stress. It's worthwhile to consult a nutritionist or your local health food store.

If you are tired, rest! If you are restless, exercise! Pushing or punishing yourself in the midst of change is torture. Trying to lose weight at such times will make you even more susceptible to internal shake-ups. Starving yourself during a time of change is a form of self-abuse. Know that the body can manage only so much abuse before it breaks down.

As a general rule, honor the temple of your soul and treat your body lovingly. The body during stressful times requires more high-quality, alive, nutritious fuel. However, taking too many vitamins and and eating too much rich food will weaken your immune system. Use vitamins only if you are worn down and need a boost.

Study the healing power of plants and herbs. They are excellent in tincture form when you are weak and need fortification. Use them sparingly so that they have impact but do not deplete the body's ability to do its own work. Sleep and rest will help you switch off an overactive mind, and please, go to bed when you are tired. Shifts in lifestyle or relationships require a great deal of energy, and if you are busy trying to please others, you will not have the energy you need for your own life.

It is not easy for people to understand what you are going through. Often people in dependent relationships, or people who do not have to worry about finances or meeting commitments, may make demands on you without understanding what you are going through. Life changes require more solitude and time for healing than usual. Be compassionate, but firm if you need time and space for yourself.

Prayer, scripture, and uplifting books will heighten your awareness of spirit, assuage your fears, and make your life better, providing a channel for love, healing, and guidance. Your spirit is where God lives within you—it merely asks to be acknowledged as precious and loved. It can guide you to happiness, health, and prosperity, and sustain you through fear, doubt, and crises.

It is worthwhile to observe the ways you handle your energy for clues about the way you live. Do you feel that the more you cram into one day, the better the day is? If so, please stop to look at the long-term effects of such a crowded schedule. Does the structure of your day really work for you? If it doesn't, please ask yourself how you might change it to give you more pleasure and vitality.

You should also take a look at your relationships, your creative skills, and the ways you enjoy yourself. Anything that augments your sense of Self will add to your independence. Anything that weakens your sense of Self should be removed from your life. Learning the wisdom to differentiate between the two will bring empowerment and freedom.

Meditation

Meditation is a powerful tool for accessing your inner radiance. It offers greater inner stability than anything I know, calming the mind and freeing up energy. It can be done virtually anywhere at any time. It is the simple act of going within to find the stillness that links you to the bedrock of your being. It's as easy as breathing.

It is during times when we are shaken by change that we make the strongest connection with the Source, that place within ourselves where we are our own best friend and inner guide. This is the part of us that is connected to the highest aspects of our being. It can release the deep knowledge of the subconscious mind to provide us with the intelligence we need to move forward. This is what I refer to in this book as "our knowing." Waking visions and dreams also help people connect with their "knowing."

I find that without these moments of inner tranquility I am less focused. They make my contact with people meaningful and rich and my activities less frenetic. I need time to be with my Self on a regular basis. It is the same as having nurturing food and water. I have come to love and trust this inner Self where I am unchangeable, yet I accept my weakness, lack of generosity, or immaturity as a part, but not all of who I am. The part of me that is the all-loving, all-compassionate Mother emerges and is acknowledged as well.

Meditation is often most difficult to do when we are caught in a difficult time and our adrenaline is pumping from anxiety. Nevertheless, it is the one medicine that is the perfect antidote to stress. It takes only a willingness to be with ourselves and look inward. Everything eventually calms down, and the mind is led toward order, stability, and peace. It feels so good and it's there anytime you need it.

Sitting for a few moments on a daily basis may be all you can do before you become agitated. As you get more comfortable, you can increase your meditation time. Don't push yourself, accept how it is for you, and let that be good enough. Of all the remedies I have used in my life, meditation has been the most valuable—it helps me know who I am. I set aside time each morning and evening to sit quietly for ten to twenty minutes. You may find that upon waking up or just before going to sleep you are the most open to meditation. Sitting or lying quietly and simply allowing yourself to be is all that is required. You can do this in planes, cars, and trains; it can even happen while you are in the subway or bathtub. I have meditated in cloakrooms, toilets, back gardens, on the street, on top of mountains, swimming in the sea, working out— any place where my need to go within was calling me. I prefer to be at home with incense, candles, the Bible, and my spiritual books. A small shrine, crystals, or photos of spiritual people or loved ones, can provide a lovely setting. The dividends of meditation are so immense they could fill a book. Meditation can ease my pain and give me answers as well to unlikely questions like where would I find research material for my books or remedies for treating specific conditions.

Meditation does takes practice. If you are willing to persevere, you will find it becomes easier and more enjoyable each time. It will tune your mind to a higher vibration so that you can look at change objectively. Meditation can stop adrenaline from pumping through your blood, lower your blood pressure, and stop anxiety attacks. It has been proven that meditation changes the vibratory frequency of the brain, slows the heart rate, stabilizes the breathing, and helps all organic systems function better.

This is the way I meditate. I begin by sitting quietly on a cushion, in a chair with a firm back, or on my bed. I light a candle because it softens the energy around me and resonates with my own inner fire. I close my eyes and take a few deep breaths. I do this until I feel my eyes begin to relax and pull gently inward into my head. I release my jaw and let my tongue fall back into my throat. I feel for any discomfort in my body and breathe into that place to let it go, using my breath to release the tension. I sit still, breathing in and breathing out. There is nothing to do and nothing to focus on. I open myself to my higher Self and concentrate on the stillness within and around me. When I am fractious and find it too difficult to be still, I examine the qualities and form of each chakra. I bring harmony into whichever center is out of balance. By the time I have arrived at the Crown Chakra I am calm and peaceful. This may be the moment for prayer. When I am done, I visualize a cross of light within the circle of light surrounding each chakra, thus closing down all seven chakras. This protects them and keeps my energy intact. I see myself sitting in a seamless veil of light which embraces me at all times.

I may offer a prayer when I am through, thanking my angels and guardian spirit, as well as the spirit of Christos within me. I acknowledge Archangel Michael and the Virgin Mary as my protectors. You can thank your Higher Self, Infinite Intelligence, The Christ Light, or Buddha. When we act as co-creators of our life with God and take responsibility for our needs, we are on our way to freedom. We may be asking for health, love, financial assistance, or release from pain. By asking, we affirm our trust that we will always be given whatever is for our highest good and greatest joy. Creating a relationship with God is our personal responsibility. If you find you have a negative image of God who deprives you of the things you want, please look at what you have projected on the blank wall of the Universal Mind. It is much better to create a loving God, a power so great it only loves and cares for us, and represents all goodness and beauty.

An active relationship with spirit helps to keep us humble and take responsibility for ourselves. When we ask for something and it starts to unfold, it is important to acknowledge and thank that creative force which has manifested our intent. It is okay to ask for love, friendship, happiness, joy, self-expression, validation, prosperity, and enlightenment. We make it right with ourselves when we ask; we make it right with God when we receive the gift, and offer up our thanks.

Energy Medicine

There are different types of energy medicine which support the immune system and keep us optimally healthy during times of stress. I am a registered Classical Homeopath. I have treated many people who were in the midst of a life change with homeopathic remedies. They have responded quickly and received the energy they needed to make healthy shifts in their lives. When we truly honor ourselves, we choose the right medicine and the right practitioner to help keep us balanced, positive, and moving forward.

I feel that the three best forms of medicine are homeopathy, acupuncture, and hands-on healing which work on ancient philosophical principles to support the body/mind/spirit. They do not have harmful side effects as do conventional drugs and cost considerably less. They are not invasive to the organism. Instead, they work gently to restore equilibrium. People trained in these disciplines are generally open to manifesting a higher good for themselves, their patients, and the planet. Conventional medicine, with its heroic doses of chemicals, can compromise the immune system, weaken the will, drain the body of energy, and leave a residue that can stay in the body for a long time. It can limit vitality and damage the delicate ecosystem required for a well-functioning body.

You don't have to like your practitioner—you do have to feel sufficiently comfortable to discuss your symptoms openly so that he or she can assess your case and give you the best treatment possible. Most holistic or energetic practitioners are concerned with the whole person, taking into account how you feel emotionally as well as physically. Your emotions help them assess your imbalance and discover the cause of your dysfunction. I also avail myself of acupuncture and hands-on healing when I am blocked. These help me find the awareness I need to make the necessary shifts in my life. After I have had a session, I can view my situation from a different perspective. Having professional support at a difficult time can make all the difference.

People in the midst of change burn their energy quickly and therefore may become exhausted and not able to replenish their reserves. Change takes its toll on many levels not just on our vitality and stamina, but on our emotions too. This drain can leave us with a compromised immunity, and our mental and physical problems seem worse. Women will start having irregular periods or stop their cycle altogether. Headaches, hair loss, bloating, and nausea are signs of stress. People can develop all kinds of irregularities and go running to physicians for immediate help. It is easy to stay dependent on drugs which pacify the terrified inner Child and make the doctor the all-powerful lifeline. What we really need is a strong will to forge ahead and find the discipline to stabilize ourselves. When a person is ill, a holistic practitioner will look into the totality of symptoms and work to balance mind/body/spirit.

When people do not feel their feelings, their energy flow will be congested, and there is no way to assess what is going on. This congested energy needs an expressive outlet, or it becomes somatized in the physical body.

People sit on their anger, swallow their grief, and choke on their anxiety. These are indications of distress—signals that they do not know where they are psychically or emotionally. They have lost the deep inner connection to their own guidance. Energetic medicine helps release suppressed feelings by freeing dormant energy. In order to bring balance back to a stressed system it may be necessary to feel these emotions which have been pushed down for a long time. Usually the body will release these feelings only when a person is ready to experience them. This could mean becoming angry or crying over past grief when we feel safe enough to do so. If at the time of change it was not possible to express these feelings, they will reappear later.

The more we become aware of our feelings the easier it will be to experience them and let them go. We gain strength and courage every time we give our feelings the space they deserve. People who live in the realm of complete rationality are frightened of feelings. They deny themselves the energy these emotions hold. Control becomes an issue because they never know where their misplaced energy is going to emerge. The clearer people can get about how they feel when something is happening, the more they will be truly in control of themselves. People who are self-regulatory do not experience obsessional disorders or acute anxiety.

People who have taken a lot of drugs are often left with feelings so undifferentiated they haven't a clue as to what is going on. They can have panic attacks and fits of rage that leave them shattered and confused. They experience memory loss and often make confused decisions. This is because the drugs have suppressed their emotions to such a degree that they haven't been able to feel themselves. Emotional energy accumulates and eventually will seek expression and release. When people come off drugs or their doses are diminished, they feel a surge of emotional energy that is often uncomfortable and confusing. Doctors do their patients a disservice by not explaining the emotional turmoil medication can cause. On the other hand, energetic medicine brings emotions to the surface so that they can be dealt with. This is one of the reasons this type of medicine works so well and so quickly. It unlocks the emotional channels through which energy travels. Chakras become congested with blocked emotions very quickly, but they can also decongest quickly when we feel our feelings and express our truths.

Consider having treatment in one of these disciplines if you are in the midst of change. It can help you conserve energy and bring balance to your life while you are stepping into the unknown. It works on a level beyond rational control, giving the spirit energy, reanimating the feeling function, and vitalizing the physical body.

Massage

Conscious touch can make the difference between feeling cherished and special, or uncared for and isolated. While you are in the midst of change, it can make a real difference in your energy levels. Massage is a healing tool which opens us to pleasure, vibrancy, and well-being. Being touched helps stabilize our emotions and soothe our tired and frazzled nerves. It is comforting, relaxing, and vitalizing. There are many different types of body work. You may wish to ask a therapist what type of massage would be beneficial. It may not be helpful to choose deep tissue work when you are under strain. You may want massage that is relaxing and therapeutic, working on those areas of tension that materialize as hard places and knots that block the flow of energy. I feel people should be stable before they take on the deeper forms of body therapy.

If you cannot afford powerful feelings in the midst of change you may wish to try aromatherapy or therapeutic massage. When people find themselves alone or anxious over stressful events, a massage may be the perfect solution to bring them back into harmony. It tonifies the body, stimulates the nerves, and sedates and comforts the psyche. Aromatherapy and therapeutic massage relax the mind/body/spirit, too. They decongest the stagnant energy that blocks a healthy response to change.

When we deprive ourselves of touch, we lose contact with our physical needs. If you don't release your tension easily, having a regular massage can help. It might become part of your regular routine for managing your energy. A massage is time focused on you, time well spent. Do find a practitioner you trust. It is a lovely way to treat yourself, and its benefits will result in a more youthful appearance and greater vitality and balance in your energy. I have massage weekly and look forward to it.

Exercise

Exercise is vital for managing the tension we accumulate in our daily lives and even more important when we are in the midst of change. It is a legitimate outlet for frustration, pent-up rage, and anger. It is a way of keeping the body strong, the emotions stable, and the will engaged.

Life is movement. The more we can bring this concept into our consciousness and apply its principles to healthy living, the more we are able to handle change. Often when people are undergoing a major transition their energy is heavy, and they don't have the vitality to move forward—sometimes they stop moving altogether. It is as though their minds take up all the energy in their systems. Their aggressive functions located in the Root Chakra become disconnected and they are unable to move forward as they did before.

Regular exercise will keep the body toned and calm the emotions. Running, walking, swimming, cycling, yoga, and aerobics will keep you fit and will also burn off excess adrenaline. Finding the discipline to exercise when you are tired or upset will moreover develop your willpower, a vital component in dealing with stress. Regular movement keeps your mind clear because the adrenaline is not pumping directly into your bloodstream, but is funneled off into physical exercise. It keeps the muscles toned, the blood circulating, and the lungs oxygenated. (One of the signs of stress is shallow breathing, and tight and blocked muscles.) There are many classes in which you can participate, many gyms and pools available. If there is nothing near you, find a place where you can walk regularly. You can always come up with some form of routine if you set your mind to it.

Many years ago I moved to a new home in the country near a state park where I found trails which I named for my emotional experiences. When I had accomplished something worthwhile I called one the Hallelujah Trail. Another I called the Never Again Trail for experiences I never wanted to go through again. It was a difficult trail, full of muddy and boggy soil where I could fall, get filthy, and scream out my anger. I found myself going there after something very taxing took all my strength and energy. There was the Beauty Trail, I Am Down on My Knees Trail, Trail of Tears, Trail of Thanks, and Trail of Joy. I never walked because I liked to get outside. It was because something in my energy needed shifting. Walking is now a habit to shift my energy, find clarity of mind, or to let go of blocked feelings.

Good Eating

The body stores precious reserves of vitality in order to push ahead in life. Feeding the body is feeding the spirit. In times of stress we need food that is wholesome and alive, that can provide us with the sustenance we require. It is difficult for the body to process and assimilate food that is refined or full of chemical additives. Food can cool us down or warm us up. Food can help us deal with our emotions. Food soothes our nerves and keeps our nervous systems functioning optimumly. Food builds stamina and nurtures our psyche. When we feed ourselves well we are saying that we are worth it.

Learning to mother ourselves and look after our most basic needs is the first step to growing up. The good mother gives the frightened child what it loves to eat, and though it might not always be healthy, the spirit knows it as soul food. Sometimes the inner Child longs for ice cream, chocolate, Mexican food, or chicken soup—comfort food. This way of mothering ourselves is okay if we are able to handle it and not go overboard, clogging our bodies with junk. It can be a tonic, reminding us of a time when we were cherished—it can provide a connection with our roots. You simply have to remember that food is medicine, and be aware of what you put in your mouth.

We may find ourselves overeating or undereating during times of change. Watch the signs. Some people starve themselves if they feel cut off from a source of love. They need to eat foods they can digest and assimilate easily: brown rice, grains, porridge, and soy milk are excellent for feeding this sense of deprivation, as are custards, ice cream, and sweet, milky drinks. If you find yourself overeating, expressing your feelings will bring a sense of control. Digesting our feelings will help regulate the physical body so that the food is assimilated.

If people are having trouble managing change on a psychological level it will manifest on a physical level, and they can experience a multitude of digestive problems.

When they are completely shut down they will barely eat, or they will be able only to digest one or two things. This is an indication that they are not handling their emotions and mothering themselves properly. When women go through the menopause it is a good time to review their diet. It is a time to review alcohol consumption, smoking, drugs, Hormone Replacement Therapy, vitamins, and irregular eating patterns. Young bodies can support abuse longer than women over fifty. In general, when our bodies start to break down in times of stress, we must take stock of our eating patterns to see if they are depriving us of stamina, heat, hydration, and potency. Look after yourself as an economic investment: eating well will save your health and give you vitality. If you think you can exercise and not eat, you will eventually break down. The body needs something to burn. Depriving yourself too long can also result in binges and other forms of self-punishment.

There are so many ways we can punish ourselves or reward ourselves with food. Think about the ways you treat your body, and you will see that you relate to food the same way you did as a child. If you need to feel guilt, a form of self-punishment, you will eat "naughty" foods or consume quantities of food. If you feel that you never will get enough love, food will become the substitute. If you starve yourself or overeat, you are treating your inner Child to the same deprivation you experienced. Eating high quality, alive, organic food is a sign of truly loving yourself.

Many therapists work with food and eating disorders. Seek help if you have an eating disorder. Feeding yourself emotionally and physically is so important it can take half a lifetime or more to get it right. With aging we usually become less driven to keep our bodies in the rigid mold we think is important, and we are better able to be comfortable with ourselves.

Rest

I don't think the points covered so far in this chapter are new to you, but what about rest? Rest means not engaging in the world. Rest is when we stop and do nothing. Rest relieves the mind, giving it an opportunity to consider new options; it gives the body a chance to stop and recharge. We especially need rest when we are faced with change. It is an essential part of taking care of ourselves. Taking time off may mean sleeping later, or taking time off from your daily routine, or staying in bed the whole day reading a good book, or looking at magazines or videos. It may mean taking a siesta in the middle of the afternoon, or going to bed early. Rest means putting everything on hold until you are ready to handle it. When you start a new business and work late nights, rest can be visiting a friend, going to a movie, or doing something that has nothing to do with work.

Holidays are a much more European idea than an American one. Americans take short holidays and usually run around blowing out their circuits. We cannot run at top speed for long periods of time without breaking down. We all need periods of recovery from demanding tasks and routines, ways to give ourselves permission to recover. I think this is very difficult for active people to understand. However, if you want to manage change with gusto, rest is something that needs to be built into your program of energy management. Who said you had to be active all the time? Learning to know when you need rest is a skill. You may think that talking on the phone with a friend is enjoyable, but when you hear all their problems it is no longer restful. You need to learn how to cut off and disengage for periods of time on a regular basis.

Every year I lead a retreat. When people arrive, they need a few days to unwind, to stop their incessant drive to which they are addicted. By the end of a week of exercise, meditation, and massage, they are quieter, rested, ready to go back to work. Retreat is a wonderful gift to your spirit. It is good to know that you are worthy of such a gift.

Support

Support will confirm that you are on the right path and doing the best you can. Such support comes in many forms: the right book at the right time, a phone call from someone who loves and understands what you are going through, a talk with someone who has been down the road you are now traveling, a group with a common goal, a well-trained therapist who encourages you when you are low. When you think about the people who have helped you before in your life, you'll be astonished to recognize just how many people believed in you and knew your worth. Support is a form of validation that you are someone who counts. It means that someone is on your side and is there for you. Support doesn't have to be rigid or intense; it can be gentle, humorous, and kind. It can come from the cleaning woman, a teacher, or a neighbor. In your immediate need, please open yourself to receiving support from other people.

When people go through changes their insecurities rise to the surface. They wonder if they are good enough, or if things won't work out no matter what they do. It is often more comfortable to hide, by not getting out there, by not even attempting to fulfill ourselves, because then we can't fail. Fear of failure holds many people back from experiencing positive change. We need support to help us overcome this negativity which inhibits our growth.

Visualization

Do all you can for yourself in times of change. Seek the inner spiritual guidance that affirms your worth and honors your divinity. See if you can find within your depths the belief that everything will be all right, no matter how circumstances turn out. Developing this belief may come from books and tapes, as well as from exercises that let you visualize your dream and honor yourself with affirmations. These work—they have a very powerful effect upon the psyche.

Visualization is seeing what you want to manifest in your inner eye. It is using your imagination to create the scenes of happiness and fulfillment you would like to unfold. For instance, when I knew that I wanted to write a book and could not afford a computer, I visualized a computer sitting on my desk. I then did everything I could to obtain a secondhand computer. I wrote letters to charitable trusts, creative projects, etc. I told everyone that I was looking for an old computer, while continuously visualizing it sitting on my desk. Two days before Christmas of 1991, I received a call from a man who said he had heard that I was looking for a computer. He was upgrading his system and asked if I would like his old machine. I felt I had met an angel. That is how visualization works. It is simple, and the key to it is knowing what you want.

Affirmations

Creating positive affirmations, saying them, and allowing them to manifest is an act of trust in yourself. This is a way that you can support yourself in dreaming who you want to become. You are making a statement to God and the universe that expresses your positive intention to create your life as you would like it to be. Remember that all wording needs to be in the present tense and positive. The subconscious mind, where positive thoughts are programmed into the psyche, only knows the affirmative and present tense. So if you say, I am beautiful and everyone loves me, the subconscious mind will record this as true. On the other hand, if you say, I am ugly and no one loves me, the subconscious mind will record that as true. The universe always and only says YES!

Therefore, isn't it better to program the most positive things about yourself? You take responsibility for how you would like your life to be and let the inner workings of the universe manifest your intention. Affirmations are consciously sending that message out which will attract your experience to you. Be clear about what you want. Keep it very simple and release it, trusting that if it is for your highest good and greatest joy it will come to you. The more you can remain positive, allowing the good to come, the more opportunity it has of finding you at home when it does show up. While you are waiting, use the time to rid yourself of negativity and let the space around you reflect your sense of order, stability, and security.

Feng Shui is the Chinese art of placement. It works on the premise that energy is always circulating around us and needs clear channels to bring us healing, prosperity, love, and friendship. It offers many tips on placing things in the right place, hanging bells, mirrors, and using the right colors. It also suggests that clearing space of stale, outmoded ideas lets the energy come to you. This old baggage congests the psyche. You can also clear the outside of the stuff you don't need in your life. Clearing works first on the inside and then manifests in your external world.

Friends

What counts is knowing there is someone on your side who understands what you are going through and is willing to give you time and attention to discuss it, someone who wants to see you succeed in making positive and life-enhancing changes.

We all need an outlet for our fears, doubts, and confusion. Good friends will not collude with you in your fears; instead, they will support you in finding your inner strength and resources to handle what you are experiencing. Good friends and a support network can provide a sounding board to help you. They will listen to you without judgment, letting you have the space to feel and think as you do. They can give advice if you require it, and they can evaluate a situation if you ask them to. However, in the end, you have to make up your own mind about what you want to do and how you will do it. Friends are there as mirrors reflecting your options without judgment or manipulation. They are not there to do it for you.

A good friend can give you a change of scenery or a day off. Ask someone to go shopping or hiking with you—whatever will help alleviate the intensity of your situation and give you another perspective. Or invite a friend to join you in something pleasant, a movie, concert, or play. Or consider clubs and organizations that do the things you enjoy. It is a good way to meet new people who share a common interest. It may be useful to make a list of the things you want to do for pleasure. You can either act on the list or not—just doing it can remind you to ease up and enjoy yourself.

The people who have been there for me when I needed help were kind, gentle, and sympathetic. Being with them gave me a sense of comfort and clarity because at such times I am not able to understand myself fully. It always helps to have a sympathetic ear and a warm heart on your side. Such people will give you the courage to make the next move and will support you when you have had a difficult day or a victory to be shared. Sometimes I simply appreciated the comfort of a conversation or a cup of tea. These make the difference between being distraught and reaching inner calmness. I have great appreciation for the friends who sensed my pain, confusion, or exuberance and provided comfort by just being there.

Sometimes we want love and attention from people who are not able or willing to give it. We feel hurt or abandoned and judge them for their inability to help us when the truth is they may have needs of their own. The best thing to do when this happens is to let go of the attachment to them, forgive them, and reclaim our own energy. Blaming others for not being there limits us and drains our energy.

I have met many people who were not capable of support, and many who were gracious and kind, willing to give me time and space to explore my inner reality, or just spend the day with me, hanging out, or do something to distract me. Usually people who offer their hearts and minds are repaying me for help they received from me and from other people. You will do the same one day for someone who needs a friend in a time of change.

If you are in a situation where you cannot think of a friend who can help, consider setting up a support group with people who are facing similar problems. It is a way of giving and getting support, and it can be very effective. It can also take the pressure off our friends and family. It may be more than they can handle at the moment.

Family

All our relationships stem from the central one—our family. Whether we are still close or not, we may need them when we are in a life change. Often we don't always know what we want from our family. It's also true that our family may have different ideas about how we should live our lives. It is essential to be clear about their limitations and expectations before we turn to them. Everything depends on the strength of the bond between you. Sometimes they can only offer you their blessings. This is a wonderful way of not interfering, but loving you enough to hope that everything turns out well for you. Times of change bring out your subconscious belief that a family needs to stick together, or that no one will love you like your family. Watch out. Your expectations may be too high. Who you are may threaten their beliefs. Too many demands from them may limit your choices.

Be grateful for the resources they gave you that enable you to deal with change. Families give us life and the staunchness we don't even know we had until we are tested. Our family gave us the material to work with genetically, psychologically, and physically. What we make of what they gave us is up to us. Acknowledging this frees us and allows us to thank them for who they are as we move forward in life.

Counseling

A therapist or healer will act as a clear mirror to your inner reality and reflect back your attitudes, ideas, and emotions so that you can see yourself with greater clarity. They can be helpful in times of crisis and should be considered as a viable tool for helping you facilitate change. Don't remain stuck with negative feelings and thoughts. Go see those people who are skilled in helping people through transitions. A good therapist or healer will not impose their ideas and beliefs, but will listen to your problems, fears, and thoughts, and then offer reflection and guidance so that you can make healthy choices. I have found such professionals invaluable. They have helped me help myself when I was confused, unsure, or grappling with something I could not resolve on my own. I respect and need their objectivity.

When we expect friends or loved ones to bear the brunt of our emotional load we risk abusing our relationships. They are meant to support us, but may not be detached enough to be a clear mirror. They are there to love and be loved, but not to be burdened with our problems. When we make them our counselors we impose more on the relationship than is healthy, and the strain can cause breakups and recrimination. The boundaries that professional therapists erect are absolutely necessary—they are not involved in our lives and therefore not attached to the outcome. Remember that a good professional will not make your problems go away. A therapist will empower you so that you will be able to deal with your situation in a mature, appropriate way.

Healing

Healing can take many forms. It can be simple hands-on healing to decongest your chakras and open places where you are blocked. Healing can come from a sensitive friend who can give you insight into an emotional pattern that is congested in your aura. Such an insight can focus light and energy on that aspect of your life. A good healer may suggest special foods, colors, or rituals which help release blocked energy. Each healer has their own unique understanding of the universal process and your energy patterns. I have met many healers in different parts of the world and found the best ones were those who could channel energy without placing judgment. I have been given wonderful healing by healers who let their gift flow over me to bring me peace and understanding.

Psychic healing definitely is useful. Try to find someone who is registered through a college of healing or a federation where there are clear ethical and therapeutic guidelines. All the techniques listed here are designed to assist you in loving and caring for yourself during times of transition. We are most vulnerable then and are likely to be overly emotional, prone to accidents, and unable to make wise decisions. We can also be at our most demanding, wanting things to go smoothly without a hitch. Unfortunately, life doesn't work that way and we need to surrender to whatever internal process unfolds for us. Sometimes it is joy and sometimes it is grief.

Change brings the past into the present and forces us to examine ourselves emotionally and spiritually and to synthesize our victories and losses with wisdom and forgiveness. Trying new avenues of help may challenge you and provoke emotional reactions. If this should happen, trust that these reactions were caused by energy which wanted to be released. Emotional volatility comes with change. Be gentle, forgiving, and kind to yourself when emotions arise and make you vulnerable, confused, or weakened. Learn to surrender to whatever comes up as something your Higher Self has given you for your highest good and greatest joy. Everyone has low times, and life changes provoke us to recognize the core of our grief. It also illuminates our life dreams that were not fulfilled. Take it as a sign from the universe that it is time to let go of old patterns and find new pathways to experience your deeper and richer Self.

Chakras and the
Human Energy System

How Change Happens

Change can be synonymous with transformation—moving from one state of conscious awareness to another, letting go of our present state of being, and moving onto higher ground. With this shift comes a stronger belief in our ability to fulfill life's purpose with ease, joy, and commitment. Each level of change, although fraught with risk and fear, can further our internal development and promote our psychological growth. In the midst of uncertainty, we face the possibility of our hopes and dreams coming true, and at the same time, our worst doubts and fears materializing. What we can do consciously to manifest these promises is to stay present in our bodies and conscious of our emotions and attitudes. This marks the shifts in our perception of ourselves as we move from one level of development to another.

Conscious change implies that we have choice. That choice can be no more than witnessing our inner experiences, or observing them with compassion. We can choose to feel we are doing our best even when outward appearances do not seem positive. Being aware of our feelings while we monitor our insights is one of the incremental steps to healing and growth. We move from one space to the other through acceptance, forgiveness, and creativity. Through this process, we absorb the degree of love and wisdom we need to move on. Choosing to be aware, responsible, and self-affirming each step of the way empowers us and creates a strong but flexible framework to which we can refer whenever we are confused.

If we are aware of our feelings in the midst of change, we will have a better chance to ride the crest of change. Working through our emotions, looking at our attitudes, and detaching ourselves from our fears help us gain mastery in the present as well as in the future. Reflecting on how we behaved in the past helps us respond in the future by simply seeing how far we have come in our growth process. Through this, we open the space in which change can happen. Putting self-judgment behind us, accepting new levels of empowerment, and overcoming fears create the right atmosphere.

Since change is ongoing, it serves us to understand how it takes place in our energy systems. Change happens in our bio-energy system through a series of conductors known as chakras. Energy moves in and through the seven major centers located in our auric field, or energetic sheath, and works its way through each chakra, creating a dynamic context for emotional growth, psychological development, and spiritual grace. This two-way dynamic draws energy down from the cosmos and up from the earth. These two movements interweave to form the vortex we call a chakra.

Energy moves from the Crown Chakra down to the Brow, then to the Throat, the Heart, the Solar Plexus, the Sacral, and culminates at the Root. It also comes up from the core of the earth through two small energy vents located on the bottom of the feet. It spirals up the legs into the spine where it starts its upward journey into spirit. When spiritual energy moves downward it solidifies and becomes matter. As this happens, our internal emotional vibrations attract experiences to us we call reality. How we think has a profound effect on our reality. As energy follows thought, we see patterns of manifestation emerge which contain the same emotional imprint as our thoughts and attitudes. This forms the basis of the experiences we draw to ourselves and becomes grounded in our everyday life as our belief system. If we think life is benevolent, it will manifest according to what we believe—it creates what we experience as change. This process can take seconds, days, or even years to unfold, depending upon the cycles of change and how receptive we are. This process is dynamic, meaning that it is ongoing and perpetual. Some cycles of change go deeper, involving a total transformation of the heart, mind, and soul. Other cycles are superficial, involving the body through physical development and maturation.

Our inner consciousness initiates the degree of change we experience. We are always the source of changes in our life, although sometimes it may appear that this is not so. It is easier to blame the stars, the weather conditions, or where we live. We may not be conscious of choosing change but, at some deep level of the soul, change is orchestrated as the fulfillment of our destiny, a pattern designated, some mystics say, before we incarnated in this lifetime. Although change may appear to be externally initiated, it always comes from our ability to draw to us that aspect of realization we need at that moment. One of the great mysteries is how our soul knows exactly what we need at the right moment for realization and learning. These changes are part of the life plan we call our destiny. Surrendering graciously and willingly makes these transitions easier. Accepting that life is good and will always give us exactly what we need is the proper attitude to adopt when going through change.

Seed patterns for our destiny are locked away in the core of each chakra. They do not even begin to unfold until we have begun to clear out the old dysfunctional patterns that weigh us down, limiting our joy and levels of consciousness. Life asks us to deal with what we have in conscious, loving, and healing ways. Without change we are unable to experience things we are meant to know. These seeds germinate when we unlock the inner world of knowing who we are. Clearing the path to these dormant seed patterns can take years and a willingness to keep on keeping on. For those people who must have a perfect outcome, who need to control circumstances and life events, this can be difficult. As we release our emotional blocks and examine our negative attitudes, it may feel as though all our landmarks are being ripped away. Things happen that are upsetting, even unexplainable—it may appear that we have lost our footing. There are two important questions we must ask. What is this breakdown in structure about? Can we manage the required change?

We tend to hold onto the ways we have identified ourselves—financial security, a supportive relationship, friends, health, and home—because they remind us of who we are. These have become our emotional money in the bank. When any of these become shaky or less than optimal, we can become afraid and full of doubt, not trusting life to take us to higher ground. We may feel we are losing our grip on reality. If this becomes chronic, we will become drained of energy and susceptible to disease and accidents.

Most people do everything possible to resist this level of change. Rather than looking for new ways to lead them on to higher ground, they cling to old patterns. Seldom do they accept change or take responsibility for what is happening. Some people will think what is happening is beyond their control, that they have no say in what is happening to them. Or they may simply not know how to respond. Some will turn to their emotions, exhausting themselves with grief, rage, or fury. Others will consciously choose to work on themselves during these times. They will recognize healers and therapists as messengers.

When we accept change we seek wholesome answers to our problems and look for new perceptions of our experiences. Getting stuck in the same old rut is a way of avoiding real thinking about the situation. Acceptance means looking after our physical bodies by avoiding drugs or anything that mutes our consciousness. It includes accepting our shadow side and probing into the inner workings of our minds to root our destructive patterns which limit our fulfillment. This helps us make change work for us. When anything negative presents itself we can deal with it in a positive way. As St. Francis says, "We learn to accept that which we can't change." By looking at the chakras as a model for understanding change, we have an opportunity to cleanse ourselves of the scars of separation, loss, and abuse. We can unleash our potential for growth, regain our power, find love, express goodness, and become masters of our lives.

The following chapters explore the seven major chakras of the Human Energy System in the context of understanding change. Take your time going through them so that you will understand how change will enhance your development. There are questions at the end of each chapter designed to stimulate your mind and give you a chance to release negative energy. They can give you the impetus to unblock that chakra and move ahead in areas where you may be arrested. All that is required is to tell the truth to the best of your ability. When you do not know the answer to any question, please pause. Remember that through reflection and meditation we can arrive at the answers to those questions. Take time to look within. Once you are comfortable accessing your inner knowing you will be less dependent on others to give you the answers that you already know.

The Root Chakra and Change

The Root Chakra is located at the base of the spine in the perineum. It relates to our fundamental attitudes about life and acts as a governing principle for maintaining the quality and resiliency of our life force through times of change. It can anchor our energy in structure and stability, patience, and order. The Root Chakra corresponds to our genetic predisposition.

It is felt that our attitudes toward life and the resistance these attitudes carry will emerge under stress. They therefore show us how we engage or avoid life. When we tackle our resistance we release energy to face our struggles and trials without falling into chaos, illness, or upheaval. So much energy is tied up in our resistance. Although resistance may have served us or our ancestors at one time, it now holds us back from freedom, empowerment, and health. Resistance manifests in the body as weight, tension, anxiety, and fear. When we release this energy we gain a sense of inner peace and security.

The energy of the Root Chakra provides the energy we need to cover the basics of life. It has an administrative and organizational intelligence that focuses attention and intention on survival. It makes sure we are grounded in our daily life and can manage our shelter, food—all the things we need to stay alive. Our fundamental attitudes to life affect the degree to which we toil for these basics. If we believe that life is hard and full of suffering we will create a life that has those qualities. Struggle is dependent on our belief in it.

The Root Chakra is also about our ties with tribe, clan, family, and community and their relationship to toil or thriving. If your family comes from a culture where there was serious deprivation you will carry this in your Root Chakra and have a weakened life force which comes from an unconscious familial attitude about your right to a good life. On the other hand, if generations of your ancestors thrived in life, your attitude and expectations will be positive and healthy. You will believe that you have every right to succeed in life. You will not have to work through hardship and difficult times because it will not be a part of your life force.

This is the center which nurtures organizational intelligence. When we are grounded in the material aspects of living we make a point of managing our lives well. Our belief in our ability to provide for our needs and those dependent upon us supports the energy of the Root Chakra and enhances its flow. The more we believe in a good life, the more energy we can put into making this a reality.

When there is a strong Root Chakra there is also a strong and determined sense that life is good. If the Root Chakra is weakened from generations of hardship, threat, or the danger of annihilation, our grasp of life will be tenuous, and we will find putting down roots difficult and frustrating. Change will be more normal than stability, and terror a part of our reality. We will wear ourselves out generating the energy required to resist grounding. We will find any situation that requires settling or that needs commitment and being "earthed," very difficult.

Learning how to strengthen the Root Chakra comes with accepting that outer change may be fast and sudden, whereas internal change is slow, requiring patience, fortitude, and courage. It demands that positive, life-affirming attitudes be integrated into the matrix of our emotional and mental fabric. Trust and faith that your destiny will unfold for the higher good helps to focus on the negativity that remains and release it.

The Root Chakra is linked with the earth's energy. In part, this is our physical connection to the magnetic core of our planet where gravity keeps us firmly planted on the ground. The mineral and crystalline structure of the earth's crust creates the gravitational field which anchors us firmly on the earth. This means that earth energy feeds and nourishes the Root Chakra, and is our primary connection to life on earth. The Root Chakra embodies all the characteristics necessary for promoting and maintaining life.

Since we have physical bodies and exist in the three-dimensional reality of time and space, all qualities of the Root Chakra relate to our physical functioning. Earth energy works on our sense of smell, a necessary tool for sensing danger and taking measure of whether something or someone is fresh and safe. Earth energy resonates with the internal qualities of patience, acceptance, security, stability, structure, order, and manifestation. These are aspects of living we cultivate when we participate in life from a grounded vantage point. Without these aspects, we are spaced out, disconnected, and dancing in the realm of chaos.

A weakened Root Chakra can be caused by disease, uprootedness, severe trauma, or loss. Although damage to our Root Chakra may have occurred in the past, it is possible to reconstruct a strong and resilient etheric center using the inner vision of the mind and a life-affirming attitude so that we can be our best no matter what our circumstances are. In order to stay anchored in life when we have experienced a major life change, we have to focus on grounding our spirit by staying centered and aware. It is also important to keep life simple, honest, and loving during times of change and transition.

Learning how to bring order into our life after a serious change is essential if we are going to maintain our grasp on life. When people's lives have been changed by trauma, loss, or separation, it is vital that they reconnect with the life force at basic levels. In homeopathy we call it bringing order into the energetic economy. Often people need to begin slowly and simply by taking responsibility for basic things, like eating every day, looking after themselves physically, and making sure that bills are paid.

Such small incremental shifts in self-responsibility reconnect us with life. As the spirit heals, so does our capacity to re-enter the flow, and before long we are back in life, stronger, wiser, and better able to manage the next stage. Coming out of the shock of change and connecting back into life takes time and patience, but it does happen. Trusting that it will do so is part of our inner work. One of the negative aspects of the Root Chakra is the inclination to despondency, depression, and self-doubt. When we affirm our right to life, we affirm our connection with the earth. Fostering these positive attitudes nourishes the Root Chakra.

The last chakra to heal is the Root Chakra because in the realm of creation we move from spirit to matter. Life cannot fully manifest if the Root Chakra is congested with negative attitudes limiting the way we connect our energy into the great flow of life. These negative attitudes though unconscious are often triggered during times of stress when feelings of hardship, defeat, and indifference emerge. These covert, niggling shadows of self-doubt limit our success and stop our emotional development. It takes a fundamental shift in thinking about ourselves and our lives to transform this energy that is locked into our roots.

Sometimes living through a life change is uncomfortable, unpleasant, and difficult, but the lessons it will teach us are absolutely invaluable for developing self-love and self-respect. It takes enormous self-acceptance to embrace the dark shadows within our psyche. Often these dark parts of ourselves do not respond graciously to the light of love.

Healing can happen on many levels of consciousness. Often the mind needs healing before transformation can take place on a physical level. Healing will begin on other, more refined levels, while internal shifts in our perception occur only as we are better able to embrace life. This work can ground our spirit and bring us the realization that life is showing us what does and does not support us. We then choose which path attracts our attention and offers the promise of fulfillment.

At the level of the Root Chakra what supports your ability to survive in life is good for you. Understanding our Root Chakra means accepting the pain of loss, separation, rejection, and abuse from our personal and ancestral past. It makes us realize that there are spiritual lessons to be learned and affirmations to be expressed. We need to acknowledge ourselves as having suffered through crisis and survived successfully.

Ultimate healing comes from recognizing that what is slow to transform and difficult to accept has its own rhythm, its own cycle, and its own karma to live out before the good can find a channel to our hearts, minds, and bodies. Owning the qualities of our Root Chakra is empowering and emotionally fortifying. There are mistakes that need to be acknowledged and forgiven, things we did to ourselves and to others that were less than honorable. We also need to understand that these things resulted from feeling unloved or unworthy.

Becoming the Great Compassionate Mother is the positive archetype of the Root Chakra which heals its most dysfunctional aspects. As we probe into our past, we can see the karma that needs transforming and the healing that needs to be administered to the fractious aspects of our minds. These are often places where the wounds go deep and the scarring is evident. Calling back our spirit means seeing the past with detachment and accepting it with love. We need to stop punishing ourselves by thinking we have failed. Self-acceptance will free the emotional energy tied to our negative memories. Invoking the power of healing comes to those who want to bring peace and wholeness to their past. Remember that staying attached to the past limits us and creates a continual leak of energy which is a slow drain of our resources and vitality.

Understanding the Root Chakra often requires looking at our family and the pathology and illnesses of its members. It also means looking at them relative to the events that affected their lives. This will form a matrix of understanding and a holistic vision of our family history. This will enable us to put together a montage of the good qualities we have inherited, as well as our tendency toward fear, denial, and doubt that we revert to during times of crisis. We are as much products of our past as they were of theirs. It is essential to keep this in mind as we look back on our histories.

Many of us come from peasant stock with ancestors who were farmers, toilers—hard-working people. This produces strong, but inflexible Root Chakras. These people, rooted in life, resist change at every bend. Their underlying attitude is that life is difficult, requiring effort and labor to survive. They may also have had problems with expressing emotion and vulnerability. Allowing pleasure probably was very difficult, if not impossible. These people, however, were fundamentally strong and robust.

People who are well rooted in life may be stubborn and determined, and they may resist any change in their lives as well as the lives of their families and communities. Change for them is equivalent to the breaking down of structure. They also may be prejudiced against people of a different religion or race, or they may feel that anyone who is not like them is alien, the other who is not to be trusted. They do not trust unfamiliar ideas or things.

So, although they are fundamentally sound, they have issues that need to be transformed. Some of these strongly rooted people may be driven by the underlying fear that there will not be enough of what they need, or that it can be taken away if they are not pious, vigilant, and hard working. They are generally not lazy or spoiled, and they have the stamina and power to get things accomplished. They tend to be realistic and practical. They are what we call the "salt of the earth."

Looking at your family history will give you an opportunity to liberate yourself of those attitudes that no longer serve you. It may be that in order to survive in the world at the present moment requires new skills of communication, spiritual understanding, and flexibility. By releasing your family's attitudes, you have a greater opportunity for development. Adaptation is the key to survival.

The Chinese say we carry ancestral energy in our kidneys. This is strongly related to the Root Chakra where the flight or fight syndrome is linked to the adrenal cortex of the kidneys. This is a ductless gland that governs the flow of adrenaline into the bloodstream. It is associated with the Root Chakra. When we are stressed or under attack, adrenaline is pumped into our blood, giving us the energy to stand our ground or flee from danger. The kidneys can give extra reserve to get something done, to survive. This ancestral energy gives us tenacity and provides us with reserves of vitality, strength, and wisdom that we can fall back on during times of challenge or change, such as dealing with physical illness or coping with the stress of completing a project. The Chinese refer to this as the Seas of Reserve and form their medical model of energy medicine around this concept. If we use up these reserves of energy without replenishing them we develop the autoimmune deficiency diseases which waste our bodies and diminish our spirits.

The Chinese look at these Seas of Reserve as investment accounts in which we can add energy by taking care of ourselves, replenishing what we use up with good food, rest, and enjoyable experiences. We can then draw upon these reserves when we need to heal from sickness or difficult situations. When we have peace of mind and are relaxed and enjoying ourselves, or take a rest from our daily routine, we are investing in the Seas of Reserve, providing the future energy to do the tasks and projects we will need for survival and well-being. It is investing in ourselves at the most profound level. This process is similar to dipping into your savings accounts when you are running out of cash. It is like running up huge overdrafts in your checking account, or paying high interest rates on a loan. If you do this for too long, you will become bankrupt.

We all need to know how to conserve our vitality for what is important to us. Giving our energy to people who do not fortify us depletes our spirit. (The same thing goes for giving our energy to things which really don't support us.) People who need to look good in others' eyes, or need to be liked by persons who rarely complement them, find that diminished energy is part of their daily experience. To burn up your vital life force because you feel you need something from others is the etiology behind such diseases as MS and Epstein-Barr, and all autoimmune deficiency diseases. Denial of Self results in weakened energy reserves. There is always a story behind these diseases which reflects a basic overtaxing of energy. This has an emotional root that stems from an underlying attitude that who we are and what we do are not enough.

Changes show us the holes in our energy, the dark spaces where healing is needed to return to a fuller, sweeter life. We can fill these holes with things that enhance our joy and well-being. What those things are is unique to each person. I call it the things that make your heart sing. Learning to accept the truth that change is necessary for our growth keeps us fluid, able to adapt.

Change can leave us feeling bereft of energy, friends, money, and clarity. Mending those gaps requires time to organize our energy and skills realistically. As we do this we become grounded, using the very qualities that the Root Chakra needs for healing—organization, patience, stability, security, structure, and a vision of what we want for a better life. We should respect how much energy it takes to make a major life change. Death, divorce, job loss, or health problems take every bit of trust we can muster to move to higher ground. We have to honor our exhaustion and develop a disciplined routine to build reserves and preserve our energy.

There have been rapid changes in our culture since the early '60s. We need to manage our life changes with more consciousness and a greater faith that the future will unfold in a positive way. If we doubt that life is good, we will totally exhaust our resources in a fight that is illusory, never to be won. It is essential to remove the fear and make change exciting and fun. Uncertainty eats away at our confidence and drains our resources. Sometimes people are so attached to being unhappy, lonesome, or uncomfortable, they like it better than being free, light, and independent. This is a recipe for becoming a victim or martyr.

These are things we can count on: it is possible to leave a marriage that doesn't work; job change is built into the marketplace; houses are bought, sold, or rented on a daily basis; schools can be changed, money exchanged, and belongings shipped here and there. It is essential to remember there are viable solutions for managing external changes. It simply means letting go, not being afraid, and knowing that something better will emerge in our lives.

Managing the internal emotional responses to change requires vigilance. It is important not to fall into indulgent patterns of negativity—otherwise we spiral down into depression and despair, both dysfunctional aspects of the negative Root Chakra. Such negativity is usually due to our inability to experience our emotions. Suppressing our feelings by holding onto anger, fear, or grief limits our enjoyment of the new and often contributes to ill health and malaise.

There are healers, therapists, counselors, and workshops to help us find a way forward during times of change or help us adapt more easily. Calling on this growing force of dedicated healers helps ease transitions. They understand the process of inner change and help make it possible for us to be in touch with our inner Self so that we can make healthy and wholesome choices. Therapists and healers can help us release those outmoded Root Chakra attitudes. Knowing that help is there goes hand in hand with a new and worthy vision of ourselves.

Why is change so difficult? Few people are connected to their inner resources sufficiently to be resilient, humorous, or grateful when they have to undergo change. Fears of change are based on old conditioning that safety comes by maintaining the status quo. Inner resources come from trusting life. When people can acknowledge their connection with spirit and their inner truth, they welcome change. They know that life is benign and will unfold as it should, always for their highest good and greatest joy. Inner knowing always comes from being in your experience and trusting your feelings. The seed of maturation and spiritual consciousness is within every person, and often is germinated in times of stress. When you can listen to your feelings you'll know the next step to take. The Root Chakra's function is to stimulate and organize our ability to survive. We need patience, stability, security, and order. We also need to be able to manifest our dreams to live our lives fully. Without these basic qualities we may fall into chaos, and our spirit may never find a home to express itself on this earth plane.

The Root Chakra is formed from the slowest frequency of vibration in the Human Energy System. This corresponds to the rhythm of the earth's seasons and cycles. It also resonates with the color red, which has the lowest vibration in the visible spectrum. The symbol of the Root Chakra is the elephant, like the Hindu elephant god Ganesh, resplendent on his hind legs with his trunk up in the air. According to myth, Ganesh is bearer of prosperity and good fortune. In India he is carved out of sandalwood, the scent of the Root Chakra. He awaits all visitors at the airport in New Delhi in the form of an enormous life size statue, as a sign of welcome and new beginnings.

The Root Chakra carries the seeds of all ancestral consciousness. If your family had generations of prosperity, good health, and stability, you should have wonderful health as well as stamina. If there have been difficult transitions to safer lands, economic reversals, illness, war, or other unsettling events which brought fear and weakening the life force, there will be limited reserves of energy available for you to use during times of stress and change. Anything which threatens your well-being will affect your Root energy and weaken you physically and psychically. Your attitudes to change will be inflexible. You will find yourself short of patience, unable to create a wholesome structure to give you safety and support. You may find change exhausting, even devastating. Change will draw on your reserves and therefore require very careful conservation of time, physical vitality, and emotional stability. This process of change is seldom honored in our culture. As a consequence, if people do not honor the body's need for rest and relaxation after periods of change, they may become ill or dysfunctional.

As children we are repositories for our family's vision of how life is and how we are supposed to be. If there is guilt or shame, or a belief that we are not worthy or good enough, we will struggle with life, unable to flourish or be nourished by our experiences. Examining our underlying attitudes frees us from the gravitational pull of past negativity. Taking time to examine who we are in the light of our family history can give us that extra bit of consciousness and energy necessary to make the bridge to a new and healthy life.

After thirty years in foreign countries I know the struggles that come with learning a new language and new customs. I know, too, that I must have a gene for adaptability from my Lithuanian Jewish ancestors who sought a better life than the one they had, full of oppression and misery. Translating my emotions into an energetic reality where I can subtract anxiety and fear out of new situations is a major part of my inner work. I want to be free to live my life as I honor my roots and move consciously on my path. My conscious choice has been to expect the negatives and affirm the positives, so that I can live in the present and evaluate my needs alongside my capabilities.

One of my reoccurring neurotic delusions is the sense I can never fit in or belong anywhere. This is evidence of a dysfunctional Root Chakra. I suspect that this is an old root pattern carried with my ancestors out of Eastern Europe. I can either affirm that I belong wherever I am, or I can live out this delusion by building a case that supports my dysfunctional belief. The choice is always mine. I know in my heart and mind that this is a delusion, but if I believe the delusion is real long enough it will manifest as my reality. I work hard to affirm that I belong wherever I choose and that I make a contribution to the lives of people around me wherever I am. I also choose to affirm that I can support myself doing what I love, surrounded by people who are loving and kind. Whenever I feel rejected or left out, I know this is the ancient pull of my roots tugging me down. Identifying this negative attitude frees me every time I find myself in Martyr or Victim mode.

Harvesting these negative ideas keeps me buoyant and vital. Accepting myself fully heals my Root Chakra and the spirit of my ancestors. Accepting my age, my body, my beauty, my intelligence, and my ability to love and heal are all part of what I must do daily, or whenever I feel cut off from the world around me. It intensifies the Mother archetype each time I embrace the person I am. It has often occurred to me I am reliving my grandparents' experience when they left Russia and came to America. They felt uprooted and knew nothing about this strange, new culture. Healing the Root Chakra requires patience, inner stability, and a dependable daily structure which supports being grounded. It also goes along with a basic belief in the goodness of life.

We learn to heal the wounds of our ancestral past each time we make a step toward unity, peace, and stability, each time we affirm that life is wholesome and will support us. In everyone's life, roots have been broken and severed. Healing comes when we choose a conscious path.

However, each time we move to something new and different, we rekindle the emotions which plagued our ancestors when they came away from oppression, escaped war, or harrowing circumstances. Fear, loneliness, and confusion are part of what happens when people move physically or emotionally from one place to another. We have to remember that whenever we make changes we have the opportunity to bring light and consciousness to the deeply buried roots of our psychic shadows. Healing always comes when we choose life. We affirm ourselves; we say "Yes!"

Change creates an alchemical process within us. During change the psyche undergoes an alchemical transformation whereby the threads of internal identification strengthen and we come to know who we are and what we are here to do. Different surroundings toughen us up, forcing us to fall back on our inner strength. Physical, psychic, emotional, and spiritual change strengthens and heals our roots, making us more resilient for the future. With change we grow new roots that are anchored internally and will contribute to our developing healthy and creative ways. People whom I have met who survived loss, separation, and trauma often emerge resilient and strong of heart.

When we look at the lives of our ancestors, what are the stories of their courage, cunning, bravery, and determination? What can we learn from family stories that spanned times of war, depression, and shifts in the evolution of human consciousness? Our ancestors not only managed to survive, they found resources. They can tell you how to manage change that no book or therapist could possibly give you. The lessons of survival and courage are built into their roots, as they are in you.

When we distill the positive qualities from the stories of our ancestors, we tap into the essence of our roots that form the base upon which we anchor ourselves. They help give us pride in who we are and what they were, and what they endured to make a good life for themselves.

They teach us to do the same, to make a good life for ourselves. Knowing who we are at a fundamental level helps to ground our spirit.

Questionnaire

Look at the following questions and use them as a guide to examine your own roots. Look at the attitudes which have been distilled from the upheavals of your family and ancestors. When you can identify any theme, remember that it also applies to you in some way. On another level, you are not your family or your past. You are your own unique person, and the qualities you carry in your genetic makeup can be enhanced or changed. You have the choice. Give yourself time to reflect on the qualities it took for your ancestors to survive their changes. The more you can understand about your roots the more you will know about yourself. As you reflect on these questions, you develop a stronger and more expanded vision of your own life.

If you were adopted, you may want to consult a homeopath to help you look at your genetic predisposition, which can be ascertained by the diseases you have had. A homeopath won't be able to tell you about your family, but can identify some of the roots of disease you carry. This can be useful for anyone who wants a clear understanding of your genetic predisposition to disease. Astrologers, too, may be able to shed some light on your ancestry if you can tell them when you were born.

The Root Chakra is concerned with the following aspects of life: birthing, family, community, clan, country, religious or racial group, work, shelter, and the ability to manifest our dreams into reality. The qualities of the Root Chakra are: patience, structure, stability, security, and manifestation.

These questions are designed as a guide to making your work richer and to give you insight into your own life issues. When you understand your family's history of survival, you will understand where your strength, courage, stamina, and natural vitality come from. If there are negative qualities, it is up to you to lay them to rest. You do this by accepting and embracing them. You may find that your ancestors were less than kind, in some cases barbaric. You need to accept that this is also part of you. Whether or not you choose to express this aspect of their being is your choice. You can heal your history by finding and acknowledging what is pure and good within yourself. There are cleansing rituals and prayers of forgiveness which can liberate you from any evil karma in your family. If this is the case and you are upset by your past, you may wish to consult a healer, priest, or counselor. Take your family skeletons out of the closet and lay them to rest!

If you find that you are unsure about a question and have no answer, you can ask your Higher Self in meditation to give you the information you need. You can also use a pendulum and dowse for the answer. Answers can also appear suddenly or in your dreams. Trust the answers that come to you. At first they may appear strange and even irrational, but you should acknowledge that they may also contain a seed of truth. You may have to sift through the information you receive in order to get at that seed.

In order to release what is blocked and congested in your Root Chakra, you may need to use physical movement to stimulate your life force. Yoga, bioenergetics, jogging, working out, walking, and dance will all help you.

You can also develop a more functional Root Chakra through your conscious intent to bring stability, structure, security, and order to your life. You can do this by meditating on the Root Chakra and visualizing the color red and a cube that represents the form of this chakra. (This information is available on audio-cassette tape and in the book *Healing with the Energy of the Chakras* published by The Crossing Press.)

Affirming that you have the right to exist and have the power to make your dreams come true fortifies this energy. Your mental affirmations will empower you and transform any remnant of the Victim archetype that resides in this center. You can change your energy into a positive and functional Mother archetype through this inner work. This energy survives under threat, strengthens under duress, and nourishes itself through self-acceptance.

Birth
- What was happening to the world when you were born?
- What historical events had recently occurred or were about to happen when you were born? You may wish to examine an almanac or history book for this information.
- What was happening to your family at the time you came into the world?
- Was there financial hardship or prosperity?
- Was the way your family lived normally changed?
- What was the global, political, or economic condition?
- Did your parents have a healthy relationship?
- Were they happy when you were born?
- Were both your parents and grandparents around when you were born?
- Was there tension between your parents? Can you identify the problems?
- What number child were you in the family?
- Where were you in the pecking order?
- Had all the births before you been normal?
- Were the other children easily birthed?
- Were they normal mentally and physically?
- Was your birth planned?
- Do you know if you were wanted?
- Did your mother have an easy delivery?
- Was your birth normal?

- How long was your mother in labor with you?
- Were you born at home or at the hospital?
- Were you breast-fed and for how long?
- Did your mother recover from the birth easily?
- Did she adjust to motherhood easily or was she depressed?
- Who else looked after your needs?
- Was there a nurse or an aunt or grandmother who helped out?
- Did your father enjoy having a baby at home?
- Did your father adjust to you, look after you?
- Did he enjoy helping with you?
- Did he love you and his other children?
- Did your sisters or brothers enjoy you and play with you?
- Is there any information that would be useful for you to explore about your birth?
- What was unusual in any way about your birth?
- If you have not had children is there something about your birth that could have influenced you not to be a parent in this life?
- Do you feel you were loved by your mother and father as a baby?

Family
- How would you describe the emotional climate in your family?
- Are they warm and inclusive or cold and exclusive?
- Do they love you unconditionally or not?
- Is their love conditional on what you do?
- Can you describe your family's attitude toward life?
- Can you describe your family's attitude toward other people?
- Who did your family define as the "others"? Were they the neighbors, people of other religions, other economic classes, other nationalities, other races?
- What did your family feel was your role in life?
- Were you expected to make their life better in some way?

- Were you expected to look after members of your family?
- Were you expected to follow the rule of the family?
- Were you given freedom to explore your own ideas?
- Were you encouraged to explore the world around you?
- Were you encouraged to get to know other people's ways of doing things, and other ways of thinking about life?
- Were you restricted to seeing friends who came from the same background?
- Were you told to go only to certain places your family felt were appropriate?
- What control was imposed upon you to do things the family's way?
- Did you manage to do things your way and still stay close to your family?
- Did you have to separate from your family in order to do things you wanted to do?
- Was your development restricted to doing what the family felt was right for you?
- Were you given freedom to do what you wanted?
- Do you feel your family loved you?
- Do you feel they supported your development as a whole person?
- Do you feel that fear and doubt prevented them from understanding you?
- Were your intellectual, creative, and spiritual needs met in your family?
- If so, how was this encouraged or discouraged?
- Do you still maintain close ties with your family?
- Is it daily, weekly, monthly, or just at holidays?
- Or do you never see them?
- Do you feel your family supports you in the choices you make in your life?
- Do they support you in the changes you have made?

- Do they support you in the failures and losses you have experienced in your life?
- What is your family's legacy to you? Is it material wealth, creativity, discipline, spirituality, physical vitality and good health, or sustainability?
- Do you know why you were born into this family and chose these people to be your closest and first links with life?
- What personality characteristics have you inherited from your family?
- What is your strongest characteristic and what is your weakest?
- What has this group of people taught you?

Ancestors and Family Myths

Every family has myths or stories about its ancestral past, about family members who were unusual, eccentric, or bigger than life. These may be tales of conquest, bravery, treachery, stupidity, kindness, or individuality.

- What myths do you know about your family, your aunts and uncles, grandparents and parents?
- Do you remember such stories or legends that were told you?
- How far back do these stories go?
- What financial and social circumstances did your parents grow up in?
- What did they do in the war, or the great depression, or the hippie days?
- How did they survive and make ends meet in hard times?
- When times were hard, what did they do individually and together?
- How did your parents meet?
- What is the myth about how they fell in love and married?
- How did your grandparents meet, or fall in love and marry?
- Can you see any patterns here that pertain to your life and relationships?
- How would you describe the patterns you see in your family history?

Loyal, powerful, ruthless, supportive, spiritual, clever, weak, boring, angry, argumentative, controlling, funny, embracing, and what else?

- What resources did your family cultivate in order to get ahead in life?
- What were their strengths?
- What were the lies they told you in order for you to follow their beliefs?
- What qualities do you have that are similar to your family?
- Where does your will come from to live a good life or do better?
- Can you see patterns of defeat, low confidence, and martyrdom in your life and your family's?
- Can you accept the best qualities of your family and leave out the negativity?
- Can you release the qualities which limit your happiness and well-being?
- Which archetypes does your family embody—lovers, warriors, martyrs, victims?
- Are there any new myths in your family?
- What myth about you and your life would you like to be handed down?

Community/Clan/Tribe
- What are the qualities which define the community you grew up in?
- How did your community maintain its identity?
- Were there celebrations and rituals which they used to mark events?
- Did you participate in these events?
- Were they important in your childhood?
- What do you remember about them?
- Did you want to participate in other communities, groups, cults, or organizations?
- Did you want to do things differently from the prescribed and traditional way?

- Did your community/clan/tribe have initiation processes where the children were distinguished from the grown-ups?
- Do you remember these initiations?
- Did you accept, and do you still accept, the teachings your community/clan/tribe stand for?
- Did you feel these teachings enhanced or limited you?
- Were you proud of your community?
- Do you still participate in their rituals?
- What rituals do you celebrate?
- What do these celebrations mean to you?
- Is being a part of a community important to you?
- What does your community stand for?
- What part of this do you accept?
- What are some of your community's attitudes that you find limiting?
- Does your community make other communities the enemy?
- Does your community have a cause?
- What events bring out the sense of community in you?
- Can you identify the elements of community/clan/tribe that are important to you now?

Class/Status/Exchange
- Which class or socioeconomic group do you come from?
- What class or socioeconomic group do you consider yourself to be now?
- Were both your parents from the same class?
- If they were not from the same class, which parent or class did you favor?
- Did you feel shame or repugnance about your class?
- Do you feel the privilege of your class?
- Did you feel that you were better or worse off than other people?

- Do you feel that your parents would emotionally support you if you moved away from your class roots?
- What attitudes did your class have about themselves, about others?
- Could you easily and comfortably mix with people of other classes?
- What was the penalty for mixing below or above your class?
- What are the qualities of your class that you identify with?
- How do you let others know what class you are from? The clothes or jewelry you wore, where your house was located, what furniture and belongings you had?
- Are there circumstances that make it difficult to define your class?
- Did your parents have breeding with no money, or did they have money with little breeding?
- Were there religious or racial barriers that limited your mobility from one class to another?
- In what ways has your class defined you as a person?
- How has it limited you?
- How congruent are your personal values with those of your class?
- Do you define people by their class, education, job, neighborhood, race, religion?
- How important are these categories to you?
- Do they get in the way of your relating to people?
- How do you perceive others who are different than you?

Nationalism/Emigration
- Are you nationalistic or patriotic?
- How would you define your sense of nationalism?
- Do you feel that your country is always right?
- Would you ever leave your country because of its political or economic ideals?
- Would you leave your country because of the weather?
- What do you consider the best or worst thing about your country?

- Are you proud of your country?
- If you have emigrated, how have you adjusted to your new country?
- What do you like about it?
- What do you dislike about it?
- Did it take you a long time to adjust?
- In what ways do you feel that you belong?
- In what ways do you feel that you do not belong?
- What have you learned about your ability to adapt?
- Do you feel you are settled into your new culture?
- What would it take for you to feel at home here?

Work
- Does your work support you?
- Does it provide the quality of life you desire?
- Does it provide for your basic needs?
- Does your work have meaning and purpose?
- If you could change your work to suit you, in what ways would you change it?
- Would you change jobs if you could?
- Would you improve the one you have?
- What would you do to provide more satisfaction in your work?
- How important is your work to you?
- Is your work toil or is it joyful?
- Do you work hard?
- Where did you learn to work hard?
- Is this a family characteristic?
- Does it come from loving the work you do?
- Or does it come from a fear that if you don't work hard you won't have anything?
- Is your work motivated by love or fear?

- Do you believe you can achieve as much by being relaxed in your job as you could if you worked hard?
- Do you do the work your family expected you to do?
- Do you do work that your family does not understand or cannot support?
- What do you sense is the reason you have chosen this type of work?
- If you are in the helping profession, what do you get out of helping other people?
- Do you feel that you have a mission and that your work serves to fulfill that?
- Do you feel this work will make you liked and cared for by others?
- Do you feel that you can enjoy your work and have a good time?
- Do you feel that you are treated respectfully in your work?
- Is this an important factor to you?
- What do like best about your work?
- What do you like least?
- What is the significance of work for you?
- How would you make your work more meaningful?

Shelter
- Do you like your home?
- Do you feel attached to it?
- Is it your own home or do you rent/lease it?
- Do you have a mortgage on your home?
- Are you able to meet the payments easily?
- How important is it for you to live in your own home?
- Could you easily share your space with others?
- Are you able to relax and find peace in your home?
- What do you like the most and the least about your home?
- Do you think of changing your home soon, and for what reasons?
- Does your home provide you with the space for your needs?

- Does your home allow you to fully maximize your creativity?
- Can you make noise, be naked, sing, dance, paint, or write in this space?
- Are you always inhibited, fearing that other people may hear or see you?
- Do you get rest and sense of security from your home?
- What is it about your home that distinguishes it from the home you grew up in?
- Is it more relaxed in your home than in your family home?
- What does your home need?
- What will make your feel more at home in your home?
- When will you give yourself what you need to be more at home in your home?

As you examine the following qualities, reflect on whether or not they are developed in your personality. These give form and definition to the boundaries of the Root Chakra. If these qualities in you are immature, developing them will build your character and help you ground your spirit. They will assist you in building the positive archetype of the Great Compassionate Mother.

A strong Root Chakra is essential for keeping us grounded, realistic, and focused on the process of our lives. The Root Chakra anchors us in the flow of life and is the foundation upon which everything we do in our life is based—how we approach all aspects of living.

The Root Chakra is the first chakra in our system to open and the last to heal. When we have cleansed this chakra of the negative attitudes carried by our ancestors and families, we begin to know that life can be wonderful and gracious. We learn a new model for liberating ourselves of struggle and defeat. We are better able to affirm our being as positive and our spirit as good, and it becomes easier to flow in life as healthy, wholesome, well-grounded people.

Many people think they are grounded because they do everything required for a successful, prosperous life. However, their lives may be based on fear and distrust. Constant fear and the compulsion to be perfect make them strive beyond their capacity. They are thus locked into the Victim archetype. What motivates them is their sense of lack and deprivation.

They can heal this center by bringing awareness to their underlying belief that life is hard and will drag them down if they are not vigilant. Their attitude depletes their energy and drains their vitality. Such beliefs ultimately do not serve them in their quest for a more wholesome life.

Be willing to examine the qualities which make up your Root center and see if you can strengthen this chakra by removing what is unrealistic and does not support you. You can also meditate on the qualities of the Root Chakra to strengthen your foundations.

Patience
• How patient are you?
• Do you become frustrated easily?
• Do you give up too soon when patience would allow you to have the things you want?
• Are you able to await patiently for your highest good and greatest joy?
• Do you try to push ahead rather than wait for things to come to you?
• Do you patiently await for life to unfold?
• Are you able to be patient even when others are pushing ahead to get what they want?
• Do you have a balanced sense of time and how it unfolds?
• What do you need in order to develop more patience? Trust? Faith? Assurance? Wisdom?
• What other qualities are linked with patience?

Structure
- What is the structure you give to your life on a daily, weekly, monthly, and yearly basis?
- Does this work for you? Is it fulfilling and meaningful? Is it too rigid?
- Is it too loose, undefined?
- Does it support you in your inner growth as well as your ego development?
- What needs to be changed about this structure to make you feel better about who you are and what you do?
- What would you do to give your life the structure which best suits your needs?
- Does your structure include time for you to do the things you enjoy with people you love and care for?
- Does the structure of your life seem too confining at times?
- Is it geared to meet the needs of those around you rather than your needs?
- What would you add or subtract from the existing structure of your life?
- How do you see the value of your structure?

Security
- How secure do you feel in your life?
- Do you feel that you have the security you need to be yourself and live the way you wish?
- What does security mean to you? Is it an inner sense of well-being?
- Is it represented by wealth? Privacy? Seclusion? Safety?
- Can you define security for yourself?
- What makes you feel insecure?
- What makes you feel safe?
- What do you do to feel secure?

- Are you careful to be safe in your home and car?
- Do you expose yourself to unnecessary risks?
- Do you feel safe when you go out?
- Do you feel you can defend yourself if your security were threatened?
- Do you feel you could make your life more secure physically, economically, emotionally?

Manifestation
- Do you feel that you have the right to have your dreams come true?
- Do you believe in your dreams?
- Do your dreams show you being happy, successful, healthy?
- Do your dreams show you fulfilling the best of your talents?
- Are your dreams about accumulating material wealth and power?
- What is the essential nature of your dreams?
- Do you feel that you are entitled to have the things you wish for?
- Do you feel that there is a better life waiting for you?
- What stops you from having your dreams come true?
- Is there anything you feel you have to do to make your dreams come true?
- Are you able to consciously create the things you want?
- Do you allow yourself to think of what you would like?
- Do you trust that your highest good can manifest when you open yourself to the truth about what you want?
- Do you give yourself the time to daydream and fantasize about the things which give you pleasure?
- Do you make lists of the things you want?
- Giving yourself this time to focus on your visions and dreams is a gift only you can give yourself. What stops you from doing this?
- Can you create an affirmation stating that you are turning your life around in the direction you would like it to go?

Order and Organization

• Are you able to organize the things you want in your life so that things work for you?
• Are you orderly in your life?
• Do you live in a messy space with clutter?
• Are you orderly in your routines? In your arrangements with others?
• Do you believe that order is important?
• Can you see the relationship between order and manifestation?
• Do you think you can improve your ability to organize your affairs?
• Are you willing to bring order into your affairs so that your mind can be creative and affirmative?
• How would you bring order into your life? Job? Relationships? Family? Spiritual life?
• Are you judging yourself?

There is no right or wrong in these questions. They are meant to guide and help you develop more balance in your energy system. Please don't judge or condemn yourself when you have an answer you don't like. It doesn't work. Look at the questions that are difficult for you and think about how you could transform them in a way that would make you feel comfortable and happy. You can use visualizations, affirmations, or you can write down lists of things you want to see happen.

The Mother archetype embraces what is dysfunctional, wounded, and handicapped in the inner Child. Integrating this archetype into ourselves teaches us to become our own good mothers. It helps us grow, develop, and support ourselves through the changes in life. It also stops us from blaming our own mothers and other people for not doing it for us.

Meditation

Hold the vision of a large red cube located in the base of your spine. It contains all the qualities and energy you need to survive in a creative and happy way. This bedrock of your physical life provides you with a foundation upon which you can build the life you want. You have everything you need to make a success of your life. Keep affirming the qualities you want to develop. Let them enhance the awareness that you are in charge, and that you can be fulfilled in your work and your relationships.

Hold the vision of happiness and health as you expand the boundaries of your Root Chakra. See the color red swirling around in a clockwise direction generating more and more energy as it turns. You are moving with life, in tune with the earth, and with yourself. Give thanks to the life force that moves in and through you for the opportunity to develop and manifest your spirit. You are unique, and you also belong to the family of humanity. Visualize your Root Chakra expanding daily. Deepen the color red. Let this cube be the symbol of your connection with life, upon which you can build a life rich in fulfillment, satisfaction, and happiness.

Affirm your right to a good life, say "Yes!" to yourself, say "Yes!" to life.

Root Chakra

The Sacral Chakra and Change

The next chakra up from the Root Chakra in the sequence of energy centers is called the Sacral Chakra, located two inches below the navel and two inches into the body. It circulates life energy at a different frequency and vibration from the Root Chakra. Lighter, more buoyant, it is more joyful and alive. It is less densely organized. It is the center of physical creativity and energy with themes of pleasure, physical well-being, sexuality, health, and abundance. It is ruled by the water element and governs our appetite or, in other words, our desires. It also regulates the flow of fluids in our bodies.

This flow, however, is controlled in part by how we experience our feelings and how comfortable we are in expressing them. When emotions are suppressed, the body swells, retaining energy in the form of fluid. The Sacral Chakra controls the flow of sexual hormones and is linked to our physical well-being and ease. Being comfortable in our bodies and allowing ourselves ease and relaxation is the essence of this chakra. It is a life-oriented center.

The Sacral Chakra deals with the relationship between our emotions and well-being, and how elated or depressed we feel about our experiences. If there is a large block in this chakra, it will be very difficult for us to be at ease. There will always be congested energy which will manifest as striving and compulsion pushing us onward. This chakra establishes the boundaries (what is enough) of our physical and emotional appetites. Its energy creates changes that make us irritable, sensual, weepy, or aggressive. When we hold on to our feelings without giving them room to be expressed or expanded, we will hold water and swell up. This is known as Idiopathic Edema, which means that our emotions contain a weight which we can palpate, a condition common to women.

When women are premenstrual and their bodies become engorged, it is because their suppressed feelings have risen to the surface. When we suppress anger, fear, or grief at any time, the body will swell in the belly, arms, ankles, or under the eyes with the sap of our feelings. This creates a state of imbalance in the body/mind/spirit dynamics. But when we are emotionally open and express ourselves, the body is balanced and vibrant.

When our feelings get suppressed on a chronic basis, our relationship to our inner nature will be stressed as well; our body will be strained by carrying the weight of our unconscious feelings. Why do we need to block our feelings and to what extent are we damaging our health by doing this?

It is interesting that when we start to express our true feelings the body moves into a state of lightness and ease. It is as if emotional expression oxygenates the body and fortifies the cell structure. Unfortunately, many people are afraid of their emotions and fear repercussions. They do not feel entitled to express themselves. The fear may stem from old, heavy baggage, carried over from childhood. If people's self-expression is dependent on the opinions and acknowledgment of others, they will be drained of vitality from giving their power to others. And if we continually forsake our own feelings in order to please other people, we damage the connection to our core and weaken our spirit. An abundance of energy linked to the expression of our inner reality is how we stay healthy.

What we find occurring in the Sacral Chakra is the need for love, awareness, and spirituality subverted by the desire for material gain or recognition in the world. In the long run this attraction to glamour will not meet our emotional needs. In suppressing our feelings, we build protective layers of energy over our Sacral Chakra which manifests as fat or girth. This is a barrier that mirrors the mind's inner need to protect itself from unacceptable or vulnerable feelings.

This suppression of emotions can lead to overeating or anorexia. It has its roots in people's attachment to superficial appearance and relationships which do not satisfy the spirit's deeper desire for intimacy and connection. Often, deeply suppressed people with a limited capacity for pleasure or well-being will shun intimacy because it is so threatening. They would rather maintain a mask than express their feelings.

The Sacral Chakra affects our sense of taste which, in turn, affects our appetite and desire for food, pleasure, sensuality, and abundance. If we believe that there is not enough of what we want, or if it is not available, we experience a sense of lack. We starve ourselves of the love and warmth we want, or find substitutes in food, sex without love, drugs, or other inappropriate acts of deprivation. A dysfunctional Sacral Chakra cannot distinguish what is enough when trying to fill the emptiness. People will seek ways of replenishing the chakra's natural energy with substitutes which appear to fill up the emptiness, but lack the real thing. A culture that has so many substitutes for food also has energy substitutes for pleasure and well-being.

The Sacral Chakra is about want. It will either want less and less, or more and more. Both are aspects of the same lack of equilibrium that is based on a sense of lack and an incapacity to know the true measure of things, situations, or people. A true sense of well-being, pleasure, and abundance is knowing what, when, and who is enough. This is a relative concept for each individual, of course. For some people, no matter what they have, acquire, or accumulate, it will never be enough—they will never feel satisfied or full. They may think that more, bigger, and better of anything will fill them up. However, it usually doesn't fill them up and they will need to seek more stimulation elsewhere.

Abundance is not about things, but about your attitude toward what you have and how you feel about yourself in relationship to things. When we feel that what we have and who we are are enough, the Sacral Chakra functions optimally, and we are at ease and content. When you love yourself, you are happy and thankful. You are fine with your sexuality, your body, and your sense of pleasure. You know that who you are, what you do, and what you have are enough. This is a state of peace both for the body and for the mind. This is abundance!

For some people a little is plenty. Abundance is the feeling that there is and always will be enough, and that life (what is) is good, another word for satisfaction. If you live in a culture that says you need to own a lot of the right things to be right, then it is easy to fall into the trap of believing if you have the right gear, the right car, the right clothes, the right mate, the right job, and do things the right way you will be happy. This is a delusion which runs and ruins many people's lives. And it is truly a delusion. If money could buy happiness there would be many more happy people around.

To have a simple life based on simple truths, you have to know what is enough for you and getting enough of what it takes to live that reality. You can do that only if you feel that you are fine just the way you are, if you accept your body, your age, your physical, emotional, and mental capabilities, where you live, and what you do. And you know that there is nothing that you have to do or change in order to be all right.

The Sacral Chakra is the most damaged chakra in our system. It is constantly demanding neurotic change and stimulation. Why is this so? The rigid moral codes that suppress sexual energy and the overuse of chemical drugs probably do some of the damage. Whatever the reasons, this center needs healing, and we begin by accepting our lives and knowing that we are good enough.

When we talk about lack we are describing a sense of deprivation, a feeling that there is something missing, that we are not enough. This is an internal experience expressed by the statement that the glass may be either half empty or half full. It's your perception that matters. Advertising and fashion prey upon the inner weakness of people with the idea that more is better, appealing directly to people's insecurity by saying that if you don't have certain things you will not be good enough. You may even be a failure if you don't live by such rules.

It takes a strong sense of personal identity to know that who you are and what you have are enough. This affirms your worth and establishes your sense that life is a rich inner process to be expressed in creativity, movement, and joyful relations. There is an old Dutch saying that "You can't have enough of what you don't really want." There is a glut of things that people fill their lives with because they are hungry for satisfaction and meaning. Feeding the gap of emptiness in the Sacral Chakra will drain your energy and create the vacuum where illness and dysfunction can breed. It can be a mental or spiritual disease gnawing away at your intrinsic sense of worth and corroding your fundamental belief in the joy of life.

Knowing what really fills you and trusting that it will come to you in the right time and place are important to your health, your energy, and your empowerment. When you know this, you will be conserving your resources for what and who really matter to you.

The Buddha said that all disease is rooted in desire. Accepting your desires as guideposts to where you want to go in life is fine. However, being disappointed in yourself for not having your desires fulfilled only weakens your health and your connection to your inner process. Accept desire and attraction as a part of yourself and give them their rightful place—not so large that they take you away from yourself, or so small that your desires become suppressed and live in the unconscious mind.

The Sacral Chakra loses energy from things that bring only momentary pleasure and prompt huge leaks of energy. A weakened Sacral Chakra can also occur from overemphasizing the physical aspects of life at the expense of the emotional, mental, and spiritual. Preoccupation with the form of the physical body can suppress weak, vulnerable feelings and soften the impetus to connect with spiritual energy. People who overindulge the physical at the expense of their emotions can also be susceptible to breakdown, even though they appear to be fit. They are avoiding their inner world for the sake of their vanity.

An expression in English that describes a dysfunctional quality of the Sacral Chakra is "to piss away money." This profligacy is based on our failure to value ourselves and on our misunderstanding of what money represents. To give over hard-earned energy/money to something that has no redeeming or lasting value suggests that we make choices for ourselves that do not honor who we are.

We piss away our lives because we haven't a clue about who we are, or where real value or meaning can be found. Sometimes we are immature and lack the tenacity and grit required to put together something substantial in life. Emotional backbone comes when we realize our intrinsic value as a person. We will know then that our knowledge, what we stand for, and what we have to offer are worth honoring and that we must claim our place in the world.

Abundance is a function of the Sacral Chakra and relates directly to our sense of entitlement, self-worth, and love of life. If we are guilty about something, we will never give ourselves the things we feel entitled to. We have to punish ourselves. We will never allow ourselves to have what we deserve. We will always have a sense of lack in this emotional state. If you don't know what is enough, you will go overboard by filling your need for pleasure, sex, and money. Such striving is simply evidence that you are trying to enhance your sense of who you are. And you will still never have enough of what you thought would make a difference. When we know our worth, everything becomes a mirror of who we are. Our friends, the things we buy, and the activities we do all become statements about how we value ourselves.

Abundance is knowing we are enough, and what we do and have is also enough. When we love ourselves, we honor our spirits and our bodies by enjoying good quality things without guilt or punishment. We also help preserve what is good around us by helping to support projects that support the earth, our homes, and our communities. Loving ourselves teaches us how to be generous and gracious to others.

If we hoard our energy, money, goods, or the awareness we receive from others through treatments, workshops, or individual sessions, we become glutted and our energy stagnates. It is vital to turn this around and give back to others. By giving we receive. People who hold onto energy become ill. This suggests that there may be a deep imbalance in the Sacral Chakra. Giving goes a long way to readjust this disequilibrium.

The way we regard and experience pleasure is a part of the function of the Sacral Chakra, and corresponds directly to our sense of being enough. If we are truly satisfied with our lives, we don't have to prove anything to anyone about our worth. This chakra plays a direct role in how we respond to others and to the feeling of joy that comes when we allow well-being to be a major component in our lives. It is important to realize that we can choose to make any life change either pleasurable or miserable. We have the ability to cultivate pleasure through healthy relationships and through activity which will promote the life of the body and the expression of our feelings. We can always choose pleasure over pain, and happiness over misery, to reflect a healthy and wholesome Sacral Chakra. The Sacral Chakra is connected to the expression of our emotions. We can monitor our responses and transform our view of any situation by asking if something or someone is pleasurable. The Self wants beauty, happiness, light, and joy.

This chakra fosters a healthy respect for our own well-being and encourages us to look on the positive side of any situation. Our sense of our own identity and our degree of positive and joyful energy feed and nurture us. We are worthy of goodness. When we choose not to rejoice in someone or something, we reflect our ideas of self-hatred, strictness, and punishment, and project these feelings onto others, too. When people hate themselves, they take everyone and everything down with them. This is the archetype of the Martyr, that level of consciousness which shuns pleasure and revels in pain.

Then again, other people may believe that pleasure is wrong and can destroy them, that they have to suffer to get through life. Negative feelings like these will influence how we feel about other aspects of the Sacral Chakra—having fun, wealth, prosperity, and ease. What we do to enhance our well-being is a statement of how we value ourselves. If we feel that the material world is still tempting, but pleasure is bad, it will require enormous effort to resist the promise that is there for the taking. And the longer we deprive ourselves, the more we will be tied into a sense of lack.

The positive archetype of this chakra is the Empress/Emperor who loves the material world and can live graciously and generously, enjoying ease, comfort, and pleasure. They know how to make and enjoy money, they love pleasure, and they give themselves time to relax and unwind. They enjoy sharing their wealth and goodness with others. They also know how to look after themselves. They respect the needs of their body and have a sense of well-being and delight. They neither punish nor deprive themselves when it comes to their desires and needs. They know that prosperity and pleasure are good for them. They nurture it and are comfortable about life on the physical plane.

Martyrs, on the others hand, have a sour quality. They do not enjoy the good and sweet things of life. Pleasure somehow eludes them. They punish themselves and those whom they associate with. Life is heavy and hard. Their energy goes into looking after others, and they give themselves very little of what they really need. They suffer from a sense of lack. The earth and the abundant life forms it contains give meaning and joy to our lives keeping us healthy. People who moan and complain a lot are not tapping into the joy offered them. They choose to stay out in the cold, away from love, warmth, comfort, and pleasure.

How does this archetype heal? By starting to appreciate and acknowledge the earth's bounties, the spirit will be free to rise higher and still enjoy pleasure and abundance. Martyrs may need to release their sense of deprivation through gratitude for what they do have. If they can accept the goodness that exists in nature, they can begin to thrive and cultivate a sense of well-being. They may need to stimulate their bodies through exercise, and develop a commitment to the life of the body.

If we dismiss our feelings they will stay buried in our gut, creating havoc and causing symptoms that take root on the physical level. Red, blotchy skin indicates suppressed anger, boils represent deep rage, bad backs manifest as a fear of abundance and a breakdown of structure. The body is a repository for all repressed emotions. Learning to listen to the language of the body gives us a directory for self-understanding. The flexibility or rigidity of our posture, even our musculature, reflect levels of emotional holding patterns. (The study of this is called Bioenergetics, a therapy which addresses suppressed feelings that are found in the structure of the body.)

Our bodies can also reflect too much food and not enough touch, too much sex and not enough heart, too much fun and not enough discipline. It will all show up as an imbalance that is reflected in the physical body. "Too much" or "Too little" are the operative words for the Sacral Chakra.

When we are faced with change, it is this chakra that responds with energy to move us forward. We draw from the reserves of vitality stored in the adrenal cortex of the kidneys, the genitals, and the liver. When energy is low because of disease, abusive habits, or overwork, it will force the body to seek fuel from the deeper levels of reserve which should only be saved for life and death situations. Keeping this chakra functional and supplied with energy means doing the things which give pleasure and promote well-being, without being overindulgent or self-sacrificing. This helps keep the reserves full of energy so that we can reach into that bank account of energy in times of stress or whenever we are destabilized. Keeping this chakra flowing helps keep the body strong. It stabilizes the emotions and brings peace to the mind and spirit. Our emotional needs for affection, love, and friendship that give us pleasure revitalize the chakra and keep it functioning as the center of our physical and emotional life.

How we feel about our sexuality corresponds to the energy flowing in the Sacral Chakra, along with our capacity to enjoy pleasure. This center is about feeling—emotional and physical. Honoring our need for sexual expression is another aspect of allowing pleasure into our lives. How much pleasure we accept is again dependent on our attitudes. Accepting that we are sexual and have physical bodies which respond to pleasure is healthy. How we choose to express that awareness in relationships is dependent upon our self-image, our body awareness, and our level of emotional sensitivity.

Sexuality is an essential component of our individuality, not something measured by glamour or fashion. It is an energy which is not dependent on weight, size, shape, color, age, or sexual preference. The truth is that we are sexual beings, and at various stages of our life that energy is channeled into relationships where that gift can be expressed, cherished, and appreciated.

What we do with that sexual energy is dependent on our deepest beliefs about ourselves. We have many choices where we can place this energy. We can use it to have others affirm our desirability. We can sublimate that energy into various activities, or we can enjoy sharing our energy with someone we love and who values who we are. We can also keep it under wraps and pretend it isn't there.

When we feel rejected or unloved, we will act out our negative attitude by getting into relationships with people who diminish us and deplete the energy in this chakra. Abusive habits and abusive people can drain the life force out of us, leaving us feeling depleted physically and emotionally. This is a form of self-abuse and self-punishment. Honoring our sexuality is a matter of honoring the needs of the Sacral Chakra, and respecting the boundaries and power of this center. We have to understand the nature of our sexual power and respect its force by choosing sexual partners who see us as people and respect us as individuals.

Most people have damaged Sacral Chakras and do not believe that what they have and what they do are good enough. They are operating on the equation that they need more to be more. The reverse is also true; if they have less they will be less. We do not need anything to be enough; who we are is enough. Filling our sense of emptiness with things which do not satisfy us or give us a strong sense of well-being causes us to lose our energy. When change comes into our lives, our reserves of energy help us face the situation directly so that we will not be consumed with worry.

When people are afraid to enjoy themselves they are generally compulsive about life and have an underlying fear of loss or death. Their energy is tied up trying to manage change rather than being happy with themselves in the moment. Even during times of change we need to stop and behold the wonders of life. People who are strict, controlling, and punishing drain the joy and goodness out of the moment and miss out on the very things they need to help them recharge their batteries.

Sometimes during difficult times we make the situation worse by trying so hard to make everything right.

If you allow change to sap your vitality because you are over anxious you will quickly wear yourself out. Doing things to please others then can add to your feelings of fatigue and stress. Nothing drains your vitality faster than fear, anxiety, or self-doubt. Looking after yourself and letting pleasure be a part of your life can help you through the most challenging time. It can help break the compulsive pattern of trying to look good. Change stimulates you to stand up for yourself, not to neglect your needs to make it right for others.

Learning how to enjoy yourself when you are alone can be a wonderful way to find the inner balance in the face of change. Many of the pleasurable things in life are very simple and easily attainable. Finding pleasure on your own will support you in times of change. It will give you that breath of fresh air you need when tension runs high. If we fail to partake of the serenity and peace of our own company, we may never be able to make the changes we need in our lives.

Sometimes the difference between stress and pleasure is how we stand and hold our bodies, or the way we breathe or don't breathe. The difference between pain and pleasure can be releasing our shoulders and loosening our knees. We have the capacity to turn anything we do into an act of pleasure. It is our attitude that determines how we view any task. We can transform what we do into a simple act of pleasure by changing our attitude toward it. Slowing your pace, or putting on some music when you clean the house makes the act one of pleasure. It is when we let go of our ideas about how things must be and surrender to the moment that we enter the realm of pleasure.

Massages, beauty treatments, acupuncture, homeopathy, and hands-on healing all work to help us relax and feel pleasure. They also work on the Sacral Chakra to give us that important edge to keep our spirits up. Pleasure is a very physical thing—when the mind is released, we are able to allow ourselves pleasure. We get energy when we are re-laxed. Our bodies then fill up with it. When we do things that make us happy, it is a reminder that we are sensual and sexual beings, and that we are doing something to bring pleasure to our lives. This strengthens and fortifies the Sacral Chakra.

If we allow pleasure and well-being to act as gauges when we have to make decisions, we will choose things that are good for us. This should be an important factor in any decision that calls for hard work and sus-tained energy—because without pleasure we will be unable to sustain our energy for long periods of time. Relationships and jobs that hold no element of pleasure do not sustain us after the first glow of romance, power, or self-importance wears off. Things that may enhance our sta-tus or make us look good in other people's eyes but do not offer us pleasure wear us out very quickly. Asking yourself if you feel good with a person or in a particular situation is a way to remind yourself that well-being and pleasure count. If we disregard these considerations, tension can overwhelm us.

Our relationship with pleasure and pain has much to do with our maturity levels. Younger people need a higher degree of stimulation than adults. When youthful pursuits are behind us, but we still demand fun and pleasure in everything we do, we have not matured. We need a certain amount of will and some rigor to bring creative projects to fruition. However, too much willpower can overwhelm the natural in-stincts of the body for warmth, nurturing, and care. We must always strive for balance.

We act as good parents to ourselves when we take responsibility for our lives, our bodies, and our health, and when we learn to accept our-selves with grace. If we punish ourselves with too much work or remain in situations that drain us, we undermine our self-determination and disempower ourselves. How we eat is a case in point. Making sure that we get enough nurturing and sustaining food is vital under stress. There are people who do not eat well or regularly, and when they do eat, they choose food without life force or vitality. If the body is repeatedly deprived of nutrients it will not deliver the high-quality fuel required for change, and we will not have the physical stamina to sustain ourselves. Without live, organic food, the body will wear down more quickly, and eventually be unable to assimilate the nutrients it needs. Many people complain of depression and a low libido when they are just low on energy. Eating well nurtures the body and makes it feel cared for.

Maintaining high levels of well-being is important during times of change. Staying in a happy and loving relationship with one's Self at all times is essential. Anything which works to undermine our sense of well-being needs to be re-examined. We need to think about what is really important to us when we are going through change. It is important to feel relaxed and have enough rest, exercise, and carefree time.

One reason we go through change is to bring more good into our lives. Change is so disruptive and demands so much energy that this must be the only reason why we would put ourselves through it. But with change we also make room for the good to come into our life.

Periods of rest and retreat give us time to reflect and recharge. Having quiet, restful moments where there is nothing to do but meditate and reflect on your life rests the mind and regenerates the body. Learning how to stop in a creative way is an art. Most people do not give themselves permission to let go. When was the last time you gave yourself permission to do anything that caught your fancy? I call it stepping out of time when I am contemplative and on my own, not making contact with the outside world. I treasure these times because they inspire my creativity, replenish my spirit, and leave me feeling refreshed.

The Sacral Chakra functions best when there is a balance between movement and stillness, action and passivity, pleasure and tension. There needs to be a level of charge before there can be discharge. Too little energy never reaches the peak of letting go. Too much energy and there is no tranquility. Finding the balance happens when you pay attention to your needs—when you slow down long enough to listen to your heart, mind, and body.

Questionnaire

When you look at these questions, take time to think about how you could consciously and pleasurably bring about some of the changes you would like to have in your life. You may want to think how you can have more energy and vitality, along with greater pleasure. To reiterate, the qualities that pertain to the Sacral Chakra are: pleasure, sexuality, sensuality, abundance, and well-being. How well you identify with these concepts will be reflected in how you honor your need for pleasure and joy.

Our sense of appetite is governed by this center as well as our ability to move and be moved emotionally. When we are open to joy, pleasure, and the good things in life we are radiating energy from this center.

Pleasure
• Do you feel you have a right to enjoy yourself?
• Is it strong and well-developed?
• Is it non-existent?
• Is it a newly emerging reality?
• Do you give yourself permission to discover new ways to enjoy yourself?
• What gives you pleasure?
• How often do you let yourself have the pleasures you enjoy?
• Do you control how much pleasure you let yourself have?
• What are your fears about indulgence?
• Do you fear that you will overdo pleasure and regret it?
• Are your pleasures physical, emotional, mental, or spiritual in nature?

- What type of pleasurable experiences do you feel most comfortable with?
- If an opportunity for pleasure presented itself to you right now would you let it into your life? What would be your reasons for saying no to it?
- Are you able to turn a chore into a pleasurable event?
- If the promise of pleasure was conditional upon you giving up something you valued, would you accept it?
- Can you be seduced by the promise of pleasure?
- Do you feel you can have the pleasure you want and still maintain your individuality and sense of self?
- Can you express to others the things which give you pleasure?
- Is your sense of pleasure strong?
- How do you resist pleasure?
- How do you initiate pleasure?
- Are you clear about what gives you pleasure and what is permissible for you?
- How much pleasure do you allow yourself on a regular basis?
- How much of your pleasure is dependent upon what others give you?
- Do you give others the pleasure they request of you?
- How would you describe the things that give you pleasure when you are alone or with others?
- What things do you remember that have given you pleasure in the past?
- What things would you like in the future to give you pleasure?
- Under what conditions are you willing to let more pleasure into your life?
- What are the rules you have about how much and what types of pleasure you will permit?
- Are you continuing to punish yourself by not giving yourself the pleasure you enjoy?

- Do you deprive yourself of pleasure for something else that matters more to you?
- When you have achieved what you want, are you willing to give yourself the pleasures you feel you would like?
- What things could you do to obtain some things you say you want?
- Can you name ten things you would like to have which you know would increase your personal pleasure?
- Do you feel it is all right for you to explore what feels indulgent or even naughty?
- Do you do the things in life which give you pleasure?

Abundance
- Do you allow abundance into your life?
- How do you let it manifest in the different aspects of your life?
- Are you able to distinguish earning your livelihood from having a sense of abundance?
- Is your sense of abundance dependent upon having a lot of material things?
- Is it a feeling about yourself and life?
- Is abundance having property, money in the bank, investments, owning your own home?
- Is abundance a full wardrobe, luxury soap, expensive face creams, a beautiful garden?
- How would you describe abundance?
- What would make you feel you had abundance?
- What would you need that you don't presently have to feel abundant?
- Is abundance to you a state of mind or a physical reality?
- What does it feel like?
- What would you have to do to allow yourself to enjoy abundance?
- What would you be willing to let go of in order to have the sense of

abundance you desire? Is this a feeling of deprivation, a sense of poverty, political ideals, victimization, or negative attitudes, etc.?

- What do you think you would have to do in your life to maintain a sense of abundance?
- Would you have to work extra hard, deprive yourself, or punish yourself to do this?
- Could you manage to feel a sense of abundance and be responsible for what you do have?
- Can you visualize yourself with a higher level of abundance?
- What does abundance look like or feel like or taste like?
- Can you talk about this vision with others?
- Does it still feel all right for you to achieve a higher level of abundance in your life?
- What negative thoughts come into your head when you think of abundance?
- Would having abundance change your life?
- Do you think people would like you more or less if you had a higher level of abundance?
- Do you think others would be jealous of you if you had a higher level of abundance?
- Would your life be easier if you had a higher level of abundance?
- Do you think you would be doing what you are doing now if you had a higher level of abundance in your life?
- How much is enough for you?
- Can you freely choose to continue doing what you are doing and allow a sense of abundance into your life?
- What would you change and what would you keep if you had greater abundance in your life?

Sexuality
- Do you enjoy your sense of sexuality?

- Do you feel good about your sex?
- Do you feel that you could allow a deeper, more enriched level of sexual fulfillment in your life?
- Are you satisfied with the level of sexual activity you presently enjoy?
- Are you open to the possibility of enriched sexual activity?
- Do you feel that you need to change anything about yourself to be more sexual?
- Are you conscious of sexual energy?
- Do you feel you have control over your sexual instincts?
- Do you feel others are unconsciously attracted or repelled by your sexual energy?
- Do you feel that sexuality is important in your life?
- Does sexuality have to be expressed in a partnership, or in a marriage?
- Is intimacy an essential component to your sexual gratification?
- Do you need a partner to be sexual or experience your sexuality?
- Do you feel you have a problem with your sexual expression personally or in a relationship?
- Do you have attitudes which make sexuality wrong, naughty, or unimportant?
- Can you allow yourself the possibility of greater sexual expression in your life?
- Can you distinguish boundaries where your sexual energy is being pulled on by others?
- Can you distinguish when sexual energy is appropriate and where it isn't?
- Can you distinguish when someone is violating your sexual boundaries?
- Can you consciously close and open your sexual energy?
- Can you tell who would be a good sexual partner for you or not?
- Can you distinguish when a man or woman is coming on to you sexually?

- Are you frightened by the power of your sexual energy?
- Can you imagine that you could have a completely fulfilling sexual experience on an ongoing, regular basis?
- What are you willing to change in your thinking to improve the way you regard your sexuality?
- Does this require that you begin to tell the truth about your feelings about sex?
- Do you feel loveable without an active sexual life?
- What would you learn about yourself if you chose celibacy?
- What do you feel the purpose of sexuality is?
- Do you feel that you need to be harsh or punishing about your sexual desires?
- How does your sexuality affect your relationship with the opposite sex or the same sex?
- What are your sexual fantasies and do you feel that you could live them out?
- Do you think that sexuality is possible without manipulation and power games?
- How do you see your sexuality now as to how it was ten years ago?
- Would you give up your independence for good sex?

Well-Being
- What does well-being mean to you?
- How do you express it in your life?
- Can you describe it in terms of how you look, feel, and respond to situations?
- How well do you look after yourself?
- How well do you look after the way you eat?
- Do you eat properly and give yourself good-quality food?
- Do you eat regularly?
- Do you live in a clean and attractive environment?

- Are your personal belongings always clean?
- Is your work space tidy and in order?
- Do you take relaxing and revitalizing holidays?
- Do you look after your physical appearance?
- Do you dress attractively and appropriately?
- Do you feel good in your clothes?
- Do you look after your hair and skin?
- Do you deprive yourself of things you like by telling yourself they aren't important?
- Are you at the beck and call of others and involved in their emotional lives?
- Are you asked to do things that you don't want to do, but do them anyway?
- What is the limit of your good will when it comes to helping others?
- Do you feel you have a right to fun and entertainment?
- Do you go out for evenings with friends?
- What form of entertainment do you enjoy to give yourself pleasure and fun?
- What would you have to change in your life to enhance your sense of well-being?
- Do you have hobbies that support your sense of fun and enjoyment?
- What are the things that you feel would enhance your sense of well-being?
- Are you conscious of any attitude in your family or culture that is contrary to your ideas?
- What are the myths about people who treat themselves well? Are they despised for being too indulgent? Too full of themselves?
- Are you attracted to people who have a high sense of well-being?
- What do you think of them?

Meditation

Breathe deeply into your lower abdomen and visualize a large orange pyramid sitting on your hip bones, pointing up toward your heart. Hold the visualization of a brilliant orange light glowing in your abdomen, strengthening your energy, and opening up the realms of pleasure, well-being, prosperity, and sensuality for you. This is the center for your joy to be felt. Make room for it. Allow pleasure, joy, and abundance to flow to you. Watch your resistance and tell yourself that you allow pleasure to embrace you and add to your enjoyment of life.

As you breathe into your pelvis, expand your sense of joy. Let it open up as you stay anchored in the awareness of your physical body. Let the joy in. Let it find its way from an idea in your mind to a living presence in your body. It is fine to feel good. It is how you want to feel all the time, so give yourself permission to feel as good as you can as much of the time as you can. Let that sense of pleasure and well-being fill you. Allow yourself to feel at one with the beauty of your physical world. You belong here and you want your environment to be beautiful and pleasant. Accept that who you are and what you have is enough. You are lovely, you are kind and good, and all good things flow to you through the law of natural attraction. It is fine to be happy, fine to prosper, and to enjoy yourself right now. Say yes to life and to yourself in every way.

Sacral Chakra

The Solar Plexus and Change

The Solar Plexus is a brilliant power source for people who know their own worth and have a real sense of their identity. A strong and resilient Solar Plexus comes from meeting the challenges of life. It can be enhanced through therapy or any inner-directed work that focuses on building confidence and grit.

Any lingering negativity or unloving attitudes you hold about yourself will detract from this vital energy. You need to be willing to build a strong sense of your inner and outer worth. This chakra is located in the nerve ganglion located below the sternum, over the stomach region. It supplies energy to the entire digestive tract, transforming what we eat into what we need to run our bodies.

On a psychic level, the Solar Plexus is the sun that radiates outward to the world, reflecting our inner light. It stands for that larger Self, the Divine Ego that attracts or repels people and experiences to us. The more we love and value ourselves, the more good comes to us. When we build a viable inner center, what is good and wholesome in life is attracted to us. That viable inner center will also resist what is negative and dark.

The heat of the sun supplies the energy for physical life and is also the source of energy we need to digest food and assimilate nutrients. This process applies to our emotional level as well—our experiences are broken down into what we can psychologically assimilate and understand in the light of our inner vision. Self-love delights in goodness, expanding and contracting whenever our personal dignity is affirmed or violated. Too much congestion in this area can lead to a chronic lack of energy, resulting in problems with assimilation and digestion. However, this can be transformed when we honor who we are and find our internal sense of worth.

The Solar Plexus Chakra is the seat of our instincts. It is where we digest life's experiences. Here we block emotions such as anger, aggression, disgust, horror, and terror, as well as fear of failure and death. It is where we feel anxiety, where our spirit feels burdened. This valuable source of energy wants to negotiate and interact with the world around it. It is an engaging and aggressive energy that at its optimum is represented by the Warrior archetype that fights for what it believes to be right. It stands up for justice and condemns wrongs, personal and impersonal. It has a strong link with a sense of personal identity, demanding respect and positive treatment. There is no victim here, only self-affirming identification and behavior.

This is an energy we need to make conscious when we are self-supporting or working in a large organization. A willingness to let go of all childish identifications is required when living from this archetype. Owning your power, standing up for yourself, and expressing your vision of reality is what this chakra is about.

We have to take the raw emotional energy we gather from our life experiences and give it a form and expression to reflect the best of ourselves. This inner effort eventually helps us embrace a spiritual dimension that will teach us wisdom. This is part of the alchemical process of turning the lead of negativity into the gold of wisdom. It comes from living our lives and engaging correctly with difficult people and stressful situations. It pulls on our inner fire.

Whenever we are in situations that diminish our self-worth and corrode our personal identity, the Solar Plexus will work extra hard to reflect our light and help us maintain our dignity and self-esteem. It has to counter negative attitudes that defeat us from expressing our innate worth. If these negative attitudes persist, symptoms such as stomach acidity, diarrhea, ulcers, hepatitis, and gallstones can develop. They represent a somatized symptom mirroring our inner conflict and weakened self-confidence.

If we perpetually attract difficult situations and cold people to us, we will eventually despair, seek isolation, or develop illness. The Solar Plexus is the center where individuality, ego resilience, and identification are important. Without these qualities we flounder in the world and become susceptible to manipulation, exploitation, and abuse.

If you have lived without having to engage in life or negotiate for yourself, you will have a weakened Solar Plexus, whereas living on your own terms builds a strong center. We all need a healthy and resilient ego; otherwise we become one of life's servants, doing what others ask without deciding whether it is good for us. We can fall into the Victim archetype every time we lose connection to our personal identity. Moreover, without knowing who we are, there is no growth or maturation. When we realize that challenging situations strengthen our character, it becomes easier to accept the effort required.

The Solar Plexus is be like a radiant sun. We are meant to shine as individuals. When we accept this as a given, our internal mechanism will always bring us what we need for our development and strength. We will know that whatever comes to us is meant to be for our highest good, even though it may not always be pleasant or comfortable. As we grow in the awareness of who we are and strengthen our energy, we are better able to make our way in life, having a happy life without following the blueprints of others. This is the center where we take responsibility for our lives. Knowing who we are is the bedrock of this chakra.

Without a well-developed sense of personal identity to affirm our worth, we can become too attached to external experiences and other people. We may seek validation from others to make us feel we are important and valuable, and thus fail to develop an internal awareness of who we are and our own worth. When we know who we are we become immune, invincible to threat, attack, and challenge.

This chakra is represented by the Warrior archetype, personified by the archangel Michael, who cuts through negativity and slays the dragon of evil. This is the chakra that defeats the malice externalized in people and situations around us. Wise people have mentors, therapists, healers, and friends who teach them how to be a strong Warrior. Sometimes in order to develop this chakra we must face tests that provoke our deepest fears of failure. Learning to handle stress, coping with uncertainty, and being brave in the face of confrontation fortify this chakra and help to develop a resilient character. What we want and attract reflects our inner being. Native Americans believe that we get the enemies and challenges that reflect our inner strength. If we are always asking to be taken care of by people or avoid confrontations, we may not be able to stand on our own two feet. If we are asking to be shown the path ahead, it suggests we can walk the road, but we are uncertain as to where it will take us. When we can feel that we are able to handle what comes to us we are demonstrating to ourselves and to the world that we are resilient and strong enough to live from a place of deep knowing and trust.

The Warrior archetype sees through glamour, insincerity, and superficial acts. With wisdom and maturity, it penetrates the veil of delusions that haunt the realms of power. The Warrior, impervious to these qualities, stands strong in the face of fear, and is an advocate for justice and integrity.

The Warrior archetype knows who he or she is and doesn't surrender any principles when caught up in the midst of change. Such a person is internally strong with the generosity of spirit to be a shining sun, independent of what is said or done. This is a masculine and martial energy governed by both the sun and Mars. The Warrior accepts reality and conflict, knowing this is a way to strength. The archetype never shuns a battle for the right or for the good. All Warriors may falter and lose ground, but eventually they will find their sense of worth. A strong identity buoys us up in the face of change better than any other quality. It also anchors us in our purpose with an indelible quality of mastery.

The Warrior always wins something personal in life's confrontations, whether or not the world sees it as a victory. For the true spiritual warrior, often consciousness, wisdom, and truth are the rewards that come after a confrontation. Even the worst situations become a means to understanding the true nature of who we are.

The Solar Plexus acts like a magnet, bringing us through the laws of attraction whatever is for our highest good and greatest joy. When we are in a difficult situation, we may not understand this, but as we reflect on our lives we can see that each difficult situation in the past brought us new wisdom that left an indelible mark on our spirit. Each loss to our being, each painful hurt identified our sensitivity; each strike on our nature showed us that we can withstand humiliation. This does not mean that we are masochistic—it means that we are made of stronger stuff than we know. Harnessing our anger, affirming our right to be, and allowing our sense of righteousness confirms the strength of this center.

If our sense of empowerment is high and our personal identity intact, we will be attracted to healthy people and situations. When we are seduced by flattery, the thrill of attention, the fashion of the marketplace, or the lure of financial gain and power over others, we will create dramas and situations that will inevitably teach us lessons about what is really valuable. We will eventually learn the importance of love, loyalty, and friendship.

One of the most remarkable things about human beings is our

capacity to fall and rebuild over and over again until the awareness of self-knowledge is etched in our consciousness. Identifying only with the external things always leads to problems. Confrontations of the most bizarre nature will appear in the guise of work, amusement, romance, finance—any field where we are susceptible to the approval of the outside world. When we begin to access our internal sense of who we are as a result of the various challenges to our self-worth, we become stronger at sorting out what is good for us.

People with strong Solar Plexus energy have a realistic, balanced ego. They weigh the expenditure of energy required in any situation and balance it against the gains. They are able to know if something or someone is worth their involvement and attention. They may despair from time to time, but when they remember who they are in the context of their inner core, they are able to transcend any circumstances, including death and disease.

Warriors are people who do not win at the expense of others. They are gracious in spirit and have enough understanding of strategy to let everyone win. People welcome the light of the true Warrior archetype and admire them and their humility. True Warriors know that they are serving others through their actions.

People who are caught in the dysfunctional Solar Plexus archetype are spiteful, ungenerous, and resentful about anyone taking their space. They make any creative event difficult by undermining the power base of those in charge because they want the limelight for themselves. These Servant archetypes have lived in the shadows of others for such a long time, they are seduced by power and pray that it will make them someone special.

Most Warriors have eventually surrendered their egos to a higher purpose. They understand that to be in any position of power takes responsibility, humility, and hard work. The archetypes of this chakra are full of light or shadows of darkness. A true Warrior nature will understand the Servant archetype and create the space for everyone to grow into strong Warriors.

Unfortunately, in a world obsessed with power, it is difficult to see through the glamour and promise of success. We are all susceptible to flattery and open to promises of love. We are immature in recognizing the dysfunctional archetype when it tries to seduce us. It takes a strong and wise person not to be impressed by what shines; it is always difficult to be immune to the sparkle and offerings of power. Manipulative and exploitive people are valuable because through them innocent people may learn to mature and protect themselves. They may develop an awareness of what is real and what is superficial. Their emotional skin gets thicker and they honor their intuition better. In short, they pay attention to their inner voice.

All the other qualities of the Solar Plexus that come after self-worth—self-esteem, confidence, personal power, and freedom of choice—are ultimately dependent upon how well we value who we are. Learning to distinguish our essence from the glamour around us and to let our inner worth shine takes a staunch belief in oneself. It is not the techniques we teach or learn, not the clothes we wear, or the car we drive that give us status—it is who we are that counts. Those external qualities may reflect a sense of how we value ourselves, but they are finite, limited, one-dimensional compared to who we are.

What does it take to know your worth? How long are you going to do things you don't enjoy, things that are beneath what you are capable of? When we don't value ourselves or honor our true purpose, we become used by people who are unfeeling—the frauds and the perpetrators. It doesn't serve us or our conscious evolution to repeat experiences of exploitation. To go within and develop a deep, permanent, and abiding love and sense of Self, as Carl Jung once said, is "steel against stone." This is an ego tempered in the fire of confrontation, forged through a strong will and illuminated by faith and love. This level of self-acceptance becomes the balm of the spirit and makes all external change possible to handle. It makes the rough edges of our personality disappear, and transforms our negativity into a positive, life-affirming light. By loving ourselves we make the imperfections right; we accept the unacceptable within, and make the unacceptable in others all right. When we anchor our sense of worthiness within our ego, we create a boundary from difficult and shallow people. By taking responsibility for ourselves, we break the ties of dependency on others to think or feel on our behalf. By making these changes we find new levels of empowerment.

When we love ourselves we become an organically permanent personality, and our development in the areas of self-esteem and self-confidence is enhanced. These qualities will take us anywhere in life and ultimately provide us with a sense of our own personal power, especially during times of upheaval and change. If this growth is done in incremental shifts, our development becomes integrated into our personalities and spirits. Our responsibility for power then goes hand in hand with wisdom, and we will understand more about the nature of service and compassionate care for others.

It is when power falls into the hands of immature, irresponsible, and greedy people that values become distorted and confusion reigns. Too much power, too soon and for the wrong reasons, keeps many people spinning on the wheel of karma as their egos inflate with disproportionate self-importance. This can destroy the health, stability, and natural goodness of people when they are given power too quickly. The old Chinese proverb that says "Great talent ripens late" is a way of saying that it takes years of hard work on one's self to step into the shoes of power. It suggests that those who do not honor themselves will abuse other people because they do not understand the responsibility that goes with their position.

When thinking about the nature of the Solar Plexus and its affinity to change, imagine the Sun and how important its light is to us. The sun's energy generates life and vitality. It stands for leadership, outward movement, connection, and the inner light of humankind. Qualities such as compassion, nobility, dignity, generosity, and strength are aspects of this center. In this chakra, when people have a well-defined sense of themselves and their ego is intact, they are attracted to experiences and people who will validate their worth and empower them. This is important because they will then be better able to manage their energy in times of crisis and change. They will not allow themselves to be drained by things and people who deplete their resources.

It can take many mistakes before you can achieve a strong sense of Self necessary to withstand the temptations and allure of the external world. What is required is that you have a sufficient sense of honor to do the right thing for yourself and others, a moral code by which to live your life, and a desire to be an individual, neither a tribal animal or a person at the mercy of their appetite.

How do you develop a strong sense of your Self? It can be done with therapy, workshops, and religious and spiritual practice. It can come from meditation or attending self-development courses. However, it is up to the individual to make the last personal steps to individualization. No course, no degrees, no external validation will ultimately empower a person. That shift in thinking happens internally. It comes with life experience and maturity. The more we examine our strengths and weakness, like any good warrior who is preparing for battle, the more we know who we are. We release the superficial and the glamorous; we strengthen our inner core, and we move out toward the world from a place of self-awareness and integrity. This is a spiritual position, and the beginning of a spiritual center.

Questionnaire

The qualities of the Solar Plexus are self-worth, self-esteem, confidence, personal power, and freedom of choice. It is your willingness to review the attitudes about these aspects of your life that will transform your energy. Look at the questions and find where you are strong or weak in the areas listed. You can strengthen your inner core by working on yourself to harvest out your negativity and begin to establish a sense of worth and value about yourself.

Self-Worth
- How well do you love and value who you are?
- Do you have a sense of how good you truly are?
- Are you dependent upon other people's good will to know your worth?
- Do you covertly know that you are worthy but play this down so as not to offend others?
- What would it take to know that you are worthy of the things you say you want in life?
- How seriously do you value your thoughts, ideas, body, and money?
- Do you need to be reminded that you are worthy of love, respect, and kindness?
- Do you need to fight for your own space?
- Do you need to create conflict to remind yourself that you are really worth consideration?
- Self-worth is an innate quality given to all men and women. Can you believe that you are worthy simply because you exist?
- Can you connect with the place within yourself where this is true for you?
- Do you feel that if you were older/younger/fatter/thinner/blonder/whiter/kinder/more spiritual/etc., blah, blah, blah, that you would then be better entitled to the kindness and consideration of others?
- Do you feel that you have to change in order to be worthy?
- Can you see that this is a delusion?

- Can you accept your worth now?
- Can you look at the people and situations in your life where your sense of worth could be better reflected?
- Does this create conflict and challenges in the ways you relate to others and they to you?
- Are you going to collude in the ways in which others undermine your self-respect? Do you believe the negative things others say about you?
- Do you feel that harboring hatred and resentment are better than standing up for yourself and expressing to others that you are worthy of more consideration, care, and attention?

Self-Esteem

What distinguishes this quality from self-worth is that self-esteem is often associated with the things we do and the achievements we have made in life. We can be proud of the things we have contributed to the welfare and well-being of others through our efforts and good will.

- Can you list the things which you are proud of having done in life?
- Do you feel that you have rightly earned acknowledgment from others for the things you have done?
- Are you proud that you can manage your life as well as you do?
- Are you proud that you can enjoy certain aspects of your life, such as having a degree of independence and self-knowledge?
- Do you give yourself the pride you deserve or do you punish yourself and degrade your achievements?
- What gives you pride in yourself?

Confidence

Confidence permeates many areas of our lives. It may reflect in everything from the way we wear our hair to the way we take risks and meet challenges. Look at your levels of confidence and ascertain where you could improve.

- Do you feel confident about yourself in relationships? Work situations? Family? Friends? Partners?
- Do you feel confident that you are good enough to do the things you want?
- Do you feel that more education, money, better clothes, or a bigger house will give you more confidence in yourself?
- Do you need to show others that you are successful to be confident?
- What helps your confidence levels? A friendly face? A kind word? A phone call from someone who cares?
- What makes you feel that you have what it takes to do the tasks at hand?

Personal Power

Personal power requires the ability to stand up for yourself in situations that may be both unpleasant and difficult. It may mean confronting your opponents and speaking your mind. It may mean making challenges a part of your life. It can also mean walking away from situations which do not serve your health or happiness.

This is where you reflect your worth, self-esteem, and confidence to transform people and situations. Personal power comes out of the direct sum of your sense of Self. It reflects a deep knowing about who you are and what you want to happen in your life. It means having the ability to stand up for yourself, even when others don't encourage you to do so. It also means, as Native Americans say, "Walking Your Talk." This is doing what you say you are going to do to the best of your ability.

- How does your level of personal power manifest itself?
- Do people listen to you?

- Are you a respected person in a friendship, a partnership, an organization?
- Do you express your personal power in an open and forthright manner, or are you ashamed to express what you know for fear of rejection?
- How would you handle your power in these situations?
- Do you give your power away to others?
- Do you empower therapists, teachers, healers, partners, colleges, but not yourself?
- Are you willing to reclaim your lost power?
- Can you reclaim your physical power?

Freedom of Choice

Once you have reclaimed your power, you are able to make decisions based upon your highest good and greatest joy. Freedom to choose is what distinguishes us from slaves. It is what people throughout the world have fought for and been willing to give their lives for. It is so valuable that personal choices have been sacrificed so that others could have this gift.

- How strongly do you value your right to choose freely?
- How often do you exercise this gift?
- Do you give in to what others want to do to keep the peace?
- Do you make free and conscious choices for yourself?
- Do you know that all healthy choices come from knowing what and who you are?
- How often do you consciously choose to do something difficult and risky because you know that you will grow and develop from it?
- Can you exercise your freedom to choose consciously?
- Do you forfeit your freedom to choose for the sake of comfort? Ease? Peace? Approval?

Mediation

As you reflect on these questions breathe deeply into your Solar Plexus. Open it up by holding in your mind's eye a golden sun centered in the middle of your abdomen reflecting light onto your liver, gallbladder, stomach, and pancreas. Affirm that you are willing to give yourself your own love and approval, and to acknowledge your own personal power and sense of value. Make space in your life and in your body for yourself.

Let yourself love your Self—the part of you which is always free, always light, and ever beautiful. This is what is permanent and whole in you and it can never be diminished.

Accept your innate worthiness. There is nothing you have to do to be worthy of love, respect, or kindness. Each time you think that there is something that will make you better, remember this comes from your delusion that you are not enough.

Grow in the love of Self that wants to find expression and be your guide throughout your life. This light will always shine and always guide you to the safety and love that is waiting for you. Thank your Self for being such a good guide, protecting you when you were under threat, challenging you to find greater truth and meaning in difficult situations, and being there for you even when you didn't want to be there for yourself.

Solar Plexus Chakra

The Heart Chakra and Change

The human heart needs to expand constantly in its effort to embrace life. The ability to accept change and to remain constant and loving are both aspects of this life-engendering center. It is through the heart that we feel love, and it is through love that we stay engaged in the process of life. To be open to life is to stay centered in one's true nature, that constant and eternal aspect of the soul. To know one's Self is to be the source of love for all things in life. When we feel we have the capacity to love we don't simply respond to what happens to us—we become the source of that love in our life. And life takes on a different meaning once we attach the quality of love to people or situations.

Change is being able to realize that there is nothing permanent, and that clinging to and anchoring ourselves in another person is not love— it's dependency. Whereas love is the freedom to be yourself and the ability to allow another person the same space. Love is the center of our lives, just as the heart is at the center of the human energy system. The heart is the physical pumping station for the body, and the haven of spiritual well-being for the soul. When we have a backlog of emotional garbage to be processed, it congests the heart, weighing it down. Emotional or physical pain is bad for the heart; it strains and weakens it. The heart wants to be light, loving, and gentle. How we perceive life's experiences affects our heart because this is where we feel the emotional energy of love. When we feel we have been accepted and loved, the heart opens and expands. When we are able to feel that we deserve love, the heart sings with joy. When we feel we have been abused, the heart weakens and contracts.

True healing always affects the heart because it is at the center of all things. Whenever we embrace the experiences that wound us, we bathe the heart in love, as a loving parent would forgive a child who is ashamed. It is the only true option for rectifying emotional pain. Forgiveness along with a release of anger and grief free up the heart to love in its natural state. Forgiveness cleanses our spirit and helps us release the pain of old wounds. By acknowledging hurt we begin the process of loosening the binding energy locked in our hearts. Forgiveness is a form of self-love where we release our pain and liberate the heart to love again. To be able to forgive those who did us harm or did not love us is perhaps our greatest power. The way the heart heals is by releasing pain and blessing those who hurt us; it sets both us and them free. The heart is not meant to be burdened with either grief or anger. It is the seat of the spirit and it requires joy, love, and peace. Whatever it takes to achieve this state honors the spirit within.

The heart has an internal intelligence that draws us toward the light. However, our thoughts and feelings control its responses. How we look at life reflects our capacity to love. This love can be rich in quality, oxygenated with awareness and joy, or it can be thin and watery, full of salty tears not shed over past pains. It can be lumpy and congested with anger, resentment, and hatred. We always have the choice to expand or contract our capacity to love. Forgiveness helps us to become more gracious, loving, and truly spiritual. Ask yourself this question. How can positive change happen if there is no room for it to enter our energy field?

The heart opens with love, laughter, and lightness. It responds when we feel love for humanity and nature. It remembers friendships and relationships where love was shared. The heart is indiscriminate about love. Its primary function is to express loving energy. The archetype of the Fool represents this level of consciousness. The Fool, depicted in the Tarot as the free man walking on the road of life, loves anyone or anything that comes into its orbit. The heart can also close with suspicion, fear, and doubt. When old emotional baggage is locked in the heart, it distorts the pure energy of innocent love and takes the form of dishonesty, malevolence, and negativity toward others. The heart will sag and break under the weight of these feelings and become weary from the burden. Its naturally flowing energy will become congested.

When we release shame or guilt, we free up our energy because we know our attitudes about self worth are now correct. When we start forgiving ourselves we understand we have always done the best we could at any given time. Then the delusions we have carried begin to disappear. These delusions come from a sense that we are unworthy or undeserving of love.

Self-acceptance strengthens the heart. When we forgive ourselves and those who have made us suffer, a new energy can rekindle our hearts, and loving relationships can manifest as healthy reflections of our inner state. Love for life feeds us and heals us. There is enough love inside us to heal the world if we choose to tap into it. We begin healing ourselves by simply letting our heart have enough room to breathe, feel comfortable, and find joyful expressions for the living presence within us. Then we can look at our patterns of fear, guilt, and shame. Feelings of unworthiness that we sequester in our hearts diminish our strength and our sense of worthiness. When we release these feelings there is room for healing, manifesting as a renewed capacity to love and be loved.

I once heard that grief runs deeper than any other emotion—it is the cause of more dysfunction than any other feeling including anger. Stored in the lungs, it can block our breathing and congest the flow of energy throughout the body. When grief is suppressed and denied, it can cut off all energy to the Heart Chakra, causing it to fail in its attempt to energize our body and spirit. This can be expressed by physical heart problems.

If our underlying fear is that we have failed to get the love we feel we deserve, grief will lodge itself in our systems. We homeopaths believe that fear manifests in the form of contradictory behavior where a person will do the opposite of what he or she really wants to do. A widow, for example, will sell the house she has lived in for many years with her husband. She will say there are too many memories there. Yet when she moves to a place with no reminders of her past, she will long for the place she knew as home.

Grieving takes time—it moves through us in stages. By denying it, we deny the love that sustained us and kept our hearts alive. Learning to be comfortable with grief and giving it a place in life makes us whole. Many people who go through divorce or separation claim that there is no appropriate grieving process for this trauma. When we leave any place or person where there was an exchange of love and energy, there has to be a grieving process before we move on to something new.

Because the heart is at the center of the Human Energy System, it can be badly affected by all unexpressed and suppressed emotions. For example, more and more people are having bypass surgery without dealing with the emotional components of their illness. A recent statistic showed that the people who can cry after surgery are the ones who heal the quickest. Using energetic medicine, such as acupuncture and homeopathy, can revitalize the heart and give it resilience by helping to release congested emotional energy. Dealing with the unexpressed emotions in therapy will also revive the heart.

We say in homeopathy that the deep suppression of physical and emotional symptoms eventually work their way to the heart. The body follows the Law of Sacrifice, meaning that the wisdom of the body is so powerful it will sacrifice any other organ before it will take disease to the heart. Heart symptoms are the wake-up call to look at the source of our emotional pain. Holding on to the idea that we are not enough, that life has treated us badly, or that we must punish ourselves, can create a burden that is the underlying cause of all heart disease, greater than high cholesterol and smoking.

When heart symptoms develop from stress, or at the onset of menopause, or after a severe upset, it is best to find an energetic, natural medicine which can take into account the emotional cause of disease. Conventional medicine can offer technical support but it cannot deal with the emotions in the same way as homeopathy and acupuncture do. Energetic medicine looks at the etiology of disease from a different level of awareness. The heart is vulnerable and delicate, innocent and pure. It is susceptible to emotional injury more than any other center of the body. Developing a strong, resilient heart is an emotional and energetic necessity.

The heart protector is known as the pericardium, the muscle that contains the heart. To honor the emotional need of the heart for protection is to acknowledge the innocence and purity of our very nature. We become healers when we open our hearts to express the love within us. Most people deny their susceptibility on this level, and yet it is the loss of real love that evokes our deepest pain. True love makes our hearts sing, reminding us of the miracle of life. As we look within at our heart's desires, we see the longing for love to be the root of our lives. Acknowledging this need transforms all our relationships. It does not matter where love and support come from as long as the feelings are genuine and unconditional. This love sparks our sense of self-worth and lets us receive the recognition and attention we all deserve.

We are either moving toward or away from love. Accepting our need for love and giving it a central place in our lives is the mark of a mature and wholesome person. Love can come from friends and family, students or clients, pets and plants, and nonphysical beings such as devas and angels who guide our way in life.

We must be willing to accept this love into our lives through prayer, meditation, and affirmation. Accepting love and being willing to do the inner work may require therapy or healing. We would be cutting ourselves off from what we need the most if we were to neglect the spirit's needs for love. No one should feel ashamed to long for love. It is basic to the human spirit. Most people have experienced pain in relationships. Wherever closeness is possible, destructive behavior is also possible. Many people are now discovering they never have experienced deep intimacy or real love. They have sabotaged it whenever it came close. This is the time to heal these old, dysfunctional wounds so that we can go forward in our lives.

Let us try to be mindful that love is at the center of everything we do. We are all touched by the words, actions, and thoughts of others. When we love, we trust that those persons close to us will love us for who we are. Their love acts as a natural heart protector. It also makes us understand how important healthy relationships are in supporting our spiritual vision of life. When we are let down by family or friends, our hearts become vulnerable.

It is up to us then to find the love within us to make up for that deficiency. We can internalize parental love and make it ours, thus creating a healthy environment in which the Inner Child can thrive. That inner world of love will help us know what and who are good for us in the world. When we are hungry for love, we can get that love only turning that longing inward to love ourselves. By loving ourselves unconditionally, we re-parent ourselves and become the parents who can support the purity and innocence of that small, unloved child crying for love and attention. Instead of projecting that need to be protected onto the world, we choose to protect ourselves.

There is an old Celtic expression that says your heart will heal when you move towards people and things that warm you. This is a good test for trusting in love. When people are starving for love, they are often impulsive and destructive. It is good to take the time to feel your way slowly into a loving relationship and refuse to compromise your ground rules. We are ultimately responsible for the quality of our relationships.

If we find ourselves in a relationship where we are constantly compromising our true self to please another, we lose something vital that undermines our own sense of worth. It doesn't support the true integrity of another person to be less ourselves. If we put up with poor behavior from other people, we are unconsciously telling them it is acceptable to behave this way though, in our hearts we know it is not. Such collusion is an inner statement that we don't think we are worth loving. Sometimes in our inner being we believe that when people treat us badly they really love us. This also perpetrates bad behavior and is the cause of many dysfunctional relationships.

The heart cheers us on when good things happen and we feel exhilarated and joyful. Watching the human heart express its full capacity for tenderness, care, love, and joy makes contact with people meaningful. When we say we want a life with purpose and meaning, we are saying we want something in our lives that has heart. Finding the place, people, and situation that have heart can take a long time. It is our intention, however, that creates the template for this to happen. We tell ourselves, God, and the universe that this is what we want, and we allow the changes to come to us. Let the heart sing its song with joyful experiences. Gratitude is the song people sing when they see how blessed they are. There may be many things not quite right, but there are many things that make our hearts fill up with joy and gratitude.

Building protection for the inner core of the heart helps people cope with the pains of life. When we don't have that protection built into our social and familial network, we become vulnerable to hurt and pain. We can build a layer of protection to shield us from abuse by prayer, meditation, affirmation, and visualization. Creating the etheric fabric of a heart protector takes a deep awareness that we are not meant to expose the innocence and purity of our hearts to abusive people and situations. When a situation becomes ugly, it is best to turn away. It's a time to make healthy and conscious changes instead. Find the grace to forgive those who have hurt you and let them go. Clinging to hurtful situations leaves people attached to pain. Exposing the hurt and replaying it over and over is another way of locking energy into the Martyr archetype. Releasing pain is a conscious and mature way of dealing with hurtful situations, ultimately leading to forgiveness and love.

Trusting that something better will come into your life is to trust that life is good. Forgiving people without dealing with the emotional energy of your experiences does not dispel your negativity, it only rationalizes fear away. A healthy heart asks that we feel our feelings and give them a form of personal expression in order to free our spirit. Tears water the garden of our souls and let the emotional roses grow. Anger has a legitimate expression by showing us how engaged and concerned we are about people or situations. Finding healthy ways to address our feelings opens us to greater possibilities for love, and frees the heart so that compassion begins to blossom within us.

We can restore emotional balance in our lives by acknowledging that we need gentleness, love, and tenderness as an affirmation of who we are. We thrive when we are loved and are able to love in return, but we need to feel safe within ourselves for that to happen. We may think we are invincible, but eventually we will be forced to open our hearts. There is no other path. No matter how seductive the glitter or the promise of power, love is what the heart knows. All people everywhere on our planet have to deal with some pain, betrayal, and negativity. We are asked by our Higher Minds to release that negativity, find the promise of light, and move toward healing. Love is the anchor that carries us through life safely. It is permanent and invincible; it will always provide support, love, and guidance.

This energy is always there. We need only tap into it. Using prayer, meditation, and reflection, we can rid ourselves of indignation and open our inner spirit. We can tune our consciousness so that it becomes a permanent source of clarity. We can rely on the inner connection to the Self to support us in times of hardship and trial. We find then that we are capable of dealing with anything because we always carry the light and love of God within us.

In the Sufi tradition they say, "God opens doors." The part of us that is a mirror of the ultimate light can see past the shadows and let the light shine in. It is our choice to let the heart open to love. This is what elevates us above our ties to power, our need for earthly and material goods, and even our need for survival. Those qualities of the lower chakras are the stuff that archetypal delusions are made from. When Adam and Eve ate from the Tree of the Knowledge of Good and Evil, the separation from God became an archetypal drama to be played out continuously in our lower centers. When we reconnect with the primal life force we know as love, it can sweep away all the shame, fear, and doubt. It can connect us to the light of God within.

Questionnaire

The qualities of the Heart Chakra are unity, love of nature, family, friends, and peace. They also include purity and innocence. Look at the following questions and see if you can strengthen your Heart Chakra as you assess where you are open, strong, and resilient, and where you are vulnerable and unsure.

Unity
• Do you feel emotionally connected to others?

- Do you feel that you are united with friends, family, and colleagues through love?
- Do you want to be a part of a group where you feel a sense of love and belonging?
- Do you feel connected to people in your town? Job? Profession?
- Does this feel good or do you miss the connection with like-minded people?
- How would you go about creating a sense of unity within your world?
- How would you strengthen your bonds of unity with others?
- Do you feel you can be united with others and still maintain your boundaries?

Brotherhood
- Do you have a sense of brotherhood that connects you with people?
- Have you ever felt that you were connected with all of life, visible and invisible?
- Do you feel that there is a bond of brotherhood with those you care for?
- Are these people on your side?
- Do you acknowledge the friendships that sustain you in life?
- Do you realize the value of these relationships or do you tend to take them for granted?
- What do you know and trust about the quality of your friendships?
- Do you sense that you are loved for who you are and for the joy that you have brought to other people's lives?
- What is the essence of the brotherhood you share with those you love?
- Is it an openness and support which allows each of you to share the best of yourself?
- Is it acceptance and respect?
- Would you be as loyal to those you love and support as you would expect them to be to you?

- What do you love and cherish about your friends?
- How are you a friend/sister/or brother to those around you?

Peace
- Have you ever experienced the deep peace that goes beyond all understanding?
- Do you know that peace is the true nature of your deepest center?
- Do you long for tranquility and harmony in your life?
- What do you need to resolve in order to find a deeper sense of peace about yourself, your relationships, your work, your finances, your health?
- Do you enjoy the moments when you feel at peace?
- Do you know where to go to find peace?
- Do you have certain friends who tap you into a peaceful place within yourself?
- If peace is an integral part of your Higher Self, do you see what meditation can do to help you experience that place within yourself?
- What gives you a sense of peace?
- Do you feel peaceful in a garden or in nature?
- Do you feel peaceful when you look at the stars and the moonlight?
- Do you find peace in solitude? Do you find peace with music?
- Can you recognize the things and people who contribute to your sense of peace?

Love
- Do you experience love in your life?
- With whom do you share the experience of love?
- Do you feel that you open yourself to love?
- Love is part of your interior makeup just as peace is. Can you find the love within yourself?
- Can you give yourself the love you truly deserve for just being you?

- Do you feel love for those who wish the best for you?
- Do you feel love for your family, friends, colleagues, or people who seek help from you?
- Can you feel love for animals, trees, all of nature, the planet, or your fellow humans?
- What proof do you need so that you know that love is who you are?
- Is it a relationship, many friends, the recognition of your family, a professional body?
- Do you need validation from an external source to know that you are love?
- Have you experienced love for total strangers, or loved someone after a short time, with a child or children, with a parent or members of your family, with colleagues, with animals, within nature?
- Do you value love?
- Do you try to develop it within yourself?
- Do you value other things such as knowledge, power, wisdom, spirituality?
- What is more valuable than love to you?
- What do you do to regenerate the flow of love in your heart?
- Do you feel the love of God or a universal intelligence for you?

Purity
- Do you recognize the place within yourself that is completely pure?
- Do you know that this is the place within yourself that requires protection and shielding?
- Can you release the idea that you are bad or evil for the things you have done?
- Can you find the place where your heart is pure and loving?
- This purity is who you are. Can you accept this point of light and goodness?

- Can you see that it was hidden, cut off from your conscious awareness until now?
- When you accept this place of pureness, it will make your relationship with yourself more gentle and loving. Can you allow this in?
- Love for yourself is not subject to the harsh realities of the world, it thrives when you generously accept what is the best about yourself. This is the place where your light shines from. Can you trust it?
- Do you want it?

Innocence
- What is innocent about you?
- Where does your innocence live within you?
- Do you recognize the part of you where you are still sweet, gentle, tender, and untouched by the world?
- This place within your heart requires nurturing in simple and loving ways. Can you recognize the best of yourself and treat yourself respectfully?
- Do you show this part of yourself to those who do not respect you?
- Do you know how to build protection for the purity and innocence of your heart?
- Where would you let your heart show, and with whom?
- Do you show your heart to your friends, family, and children?
- Do you show this side of yourself to your co-workers?
- How do you protect this very delicate aspect of yourself?
- Do you value yourself enough to avoid situations where you are disgraced, or not treated with respect?
- Can you love yourself enough to handle the hurt and unconsciousness around you without blaming others?

Meditation

As you reflect on these questions visualize a large green, crescent moon which protects the delicate energy of your heart. This moon covers the front of your chest and your upper back, going from shoulder blade to shoulder blade. It will shield your heart from the hurt and abuse that exists in the world. It will protect you and give you comfort in times of distress. It nurtures the innocence and purity of your own heart.

Imagine that God's love for you is stored within your own heart. Begin to strip away the protective cover that you have constructed to shield yourself from the hurt of others. Look within your heart and see the fire of love burning as a constant flame that can kindle your spirit. Look within and sit for a moment with this flame. Know that this is God shining within you.

Allow your breath to find its rhythm and gently release any tension around your heart. This is the part of you where love lives. It is where you are touched, and where you offer love to others. Find your warmth and feel the glow of your own love. You can be at peace now knowing that love lives within you. Be at peace with yourself and your fellow brothers and sisters. Know that all is well within you as you go forward in life.

Let yourself feel that you are safe to feel the love within you. There is nothing you have to do. There is no one there who will take anything away from you. Just be still and feel safe.

Heart Chakra

The Throat Chakra and Change

The Throat Chakra is the bridge between the love emanating from the human heart and the wisdom of the intellect. It is the vehicle for our feelings and thoughts to express themselves. It is physically and energetically the mirror of the Sacral Chakra where we are able to connect deeply with the wisdom of the body. At the Throat Chakra we express love, joy, hate, fear, and our highest spiritual aspirations. Ideas, feelings, and opinions all find form in this center. Our voices express our levels of both ease and tension, resonating with the energy of our vitality and our connection with our inner nature. As we moan, groan, sigh, laugh, or shout, the timbre and pitch of our intonations and our inflections of speech reflect where we are open or blocked. Our silences, too, reflect our inner state and how we feel about the world around us.

Without speech, we could not engage with others. It is the way we clarify, for ourselves and for others, what we want, where we wish to go, and how we hope to manifest our desires. When we fail to speak out for ourselves, we become dependent upon others to tell us what we want. If we have suppressed our hopes and desires for a very long time, perhaps we are hoping that others can read our minds. This suppression, the resulting denial, and the childish hope that other people will know what we want and need will cripple us. Whereas speech frees us, enabling us to live our lives and express our thoughts, ideas, and feelings.

Because of the Throat Chakra's location and function, it is the most vulnerable of all our energy centers. This is partly because the throat is physically exposed, not protected by muscle or bone. It is sensitive to heat, cold, chill, drafts, and moisture. Children who are shy or emotionally damaged protect their Throat Chakras by tucking in their chins over their throats, indicating that they are afraid to speak out. In some peasant cultures people wrap their throats with scarves while they work as protection from sun, wind, and drafts. We decorate our necks with jewelry to enhance our beauty and display our wealth, or as symbols that we have a connection to an idea, a person, a relationship.

What is verbally expressed with words is our conscious intention. What is expressed with sighs, tight chins and jaws, and rigid necks is suppressed energy, indication of feelings not expressed openly.

So many things can destroy the energy of this chakra. Lying, malicious gossip, and criticism are ways in which the positive, wholesome energy that has moved up from the lower centers can be leached from the system. Such negative stuff keeps people linked to the lower chakras and keeps them out of touch with their higher truths.

How well we express our truth is measured by the way we communicate with others. We can "small talk" or we can get down to the nitty-gritty of what is going on with us emotionally. Our choice depends on how safe we feel and how strongly we value our experience. When we are given the opportunity to communicate our feelings honestly, how do we feel sharing our truth with others? We may think it is a good idea, but we may not do so because we fear judgment, censorship, or even rejection.

Most people are not prepared to express the depth of their feelings. They choose safety rather than honesty. Their Throat Chakras then become congested with energy that eventually becomes stagnant. By the time energy reaches the throat, it is highly refined. If it is not expressed, other forms of creative expression can be hindered. This, in part, is where musicians, artists, actors, and writers are made.

Expressing our truth can be fraught with danger and terror. We can be easily misinterpreted or seen as boastful, particularly if we have thoughts which do not fit into the general belief system. But there are distinct advantages in saying our truth. By expressing ourselves openly and truthfully, our intentions are focused and understood. We are expressing our feelings clearly to others. Communication is what distinguishes people from the herd, but most people do not want to express anything other than what they think others want to hear.

In the U.K., for example, people wear masks as a mark of refinement. It is socially and politically correct not to show one's true face. Communication then becomes very difficult, creating a sense of solitude and isolation. In America, feelings are more openly expressed, both personally and in the media. People share their emotions easily with total strangers without any desire to be close in any other way. Perhaps this happens because of what America is, people from many different cultures coming to the same land and sharing the same space. There is an underlying need here to be understood, although not necessarily to connect.

Both Britain and America share a common language, but are at opposite ends of the spectrum of personal expression. It is worth noting that by giving either too little or too much we can hide our true nature from others. We can cover our feelings by saying anything that comes to mind, or anything we think others want to hear. There is a third way of hiding our feelings—limiting our conversation to polite comments.

How do we feel about sharing and expressing our inner nature? If we feel we are not worthy of love, respect, or kindness, we will believe that our feelings aren't important and therefore avoid sharing our innermost Self with people close to us. Such an attitude can kill intimacy with a friend or loved one. It can also lead to isolation, loneliness, and alienation.

There are probably many other ways people can short circuit intimacy. They may want their partners to know what they want without having to ask for it—like children expecting their parents to read their minds. As mature adults, we need to be responsible, we need to find the courage to express what we feel, even if what we say may not always be acceptable to others. It is especially important during times of change and transition to speak out and voice our needs and fears. It helps us master change.

There are many games played out around truthful expression. For instance, when you speak your truth, you may be attacked for the way you say it. This deflects energy from the subject matter and becomes an attack on you. Many people avoid confrontations or situations because of fear—they do not feel safe sharing their emotions.

There are many ways we limit our personal growth and internal development by not speaking out. We choke on our feelings and suffer because we believe we have no legitimate right to expression. Our mind can become deluded into thinking that there is no one who will listen or understand us. This is a source of major dysfunction. It generally stems from childhood patterns where our thoughts and feelings were completely ignored or disregarded. Few adults are able or willing to look at this past humiliation openly—it is too painful.

Any time we suppress our truth, we are helpless in a relationship that has undercurrents of manipulation. We can become victimized by what is not said, as much as by what is said. If someone loves you and cares about you he or she will want to know what you have to say. This includes personal feelings as well as opinions. Expression is as vital to a relationship as respect for what someone thinks and feels. We may not always like what people close to us say, but we must respect their right to express it.

We are drawn to people by their ideas and their thoughts. We revere poets, philosophers, and writers because they dare to speak their truth. If we think that we would not be respected or loved if we did likewise, we are looking at a dysfunctional relationship. Toeing the line and being "good" may keep us safe, but does nothing to serve our psychological development. Being able to express our anger and feel safe at the same time, being able to share our grief and humor—this is what binds us in love, friendship, and brotherhood. On the other hand, bonding too quickly, not taking time to get to know if someone is trustworthy or genuine, is a sign of immaturity and desperation.

It is easy to be drawn to people who promise us love or friendship, or tell us things we want to hear. We can be seriously hurt and even damaged by people who know how to manipulate us with words. We have to listen to our inner guidance. We have to find the balance between what is said and what we feel is right. This takes maturity and we don't get it right all the time. But our sense of truth does develop and become stronger with time and experience so that we will be better able to discriminate between what and who is right for us.

The Throat Chakras can become dysfunctional from an overwhelming fear of rejection. People avoid speaking their truths because they fear they will have no friends at all. This fear limits truthful expression and creates what therapists call a hidden agenda. This is when we speak the words that are expected of us, but actually mean something else. Rooting out hidden agendas makes for wholesome relationships. It is equivalent to putting your cards on the table, being willing to speak your truth. When the avenue for clear and honest expression becomes blocked, energy becomes subverted into unconscious negativity. For example, if you can't express anger you may do something to show that you are angry, like break something of value.

Most adults are not trained to accept rejection, nor are we comfortable with expressing our truth. This is an area that needs work.

Professional actors are very skilled in dealing with rejection. When actors audition for a role they put their best efforts forward, but are often rejected because they aren't what someone had in mind for the part. A professional will understand this and move on to the next audition, letting go of his attachment to the part. If we can become steeled against rejection, we will understand we were not right for that part, we were not the person someone else had in mind.

My friend Patricia Brown is a professional actress. She speaks about auditioning for a part as doing the best you can, and then letting go of any attachment to the outcome. She says that if you desire or covet a role it will make you tense, nervous—unable to go on to the next audition. She adds that if you are a professional you do not become jealous, envious, or nasty about roles you don't get. We should learn not to take rejection personally. It will free you to move forward to the part that may be right for you. She trusts that life will bring her the right roles that will allow her to do and be her best.

If we had this philosophy about our personal lives, we would be able to see when situations, jobs, or relationships are not right for us without taking offense when we have been rejected. We would not be hurt when we are told that we are not right for a relationship. And we would be better able to find people who are right for us because we would not be so attached to the outcome. Inevitably, we would be able to accept life more easily and liberate energy that could be used for our creativity. The right job or relationship will come along when you are ready for it. This is called having faith. If you are able to relax and wait, you will not be dependent upon other people's reactions as a sign of your personal worth.

When people are caught in the trap of their unexpressed negativity, their voices are brittle, their smiles forced, and their actions reveal that they are caught by the trap of unexpressed feelings. Because of such repression, they may harbor anger and resentment about situations that have long since passed. This is the energy that thins blood vessel walls, raises tension to stress levels, and eats away at the lining of stomachs. This energy wants to be released in conscious ways that direct awareness toward a spiritual end.

Learning to release negativity is therapeutic and fosters an affirmative philosophy to help us during times of change. If we do not forgive those who cause us pain and suffering and do not express our anger in a nonviolent way, the energy of those feelings is then suppressed in our bodies where it causes damage. By expressing our feelings we open a true path to forgiveness. When we forgive ourselves and others we develop a spiritual basis for living.

When we integrate our spirituality with our awareness about energy flow in our bodies, we give our feelings a legitimate space where they can be expressed. This practice frees our energy and opens our minds, throats, and hearts. We learn to be comfortable with the shadow side of ourselves. So often when we don't express ourselves, we become depressed with sadness, and congested with anger, and we make ourselves sick as we blame others for the wrongs that happened to us. We strip away our inner peace and erode our tranquility by holding on to negative, heavy feelings. This reduces our energy and limits our capacity to deal with change.

Expressing our feelings is the function of the Throat Chakra. People who are not prepared to deal with emotional energy often have problems with their throats, mouth, teeth, and ears. When we limit the flow of energy by blocking our expression, there is insufficient energy to feed these areas of the body, and energy has a difficult time reaching the higher centers of the mind. If there are energy leaks in the Throat Chakra because of suppression, negative energy will stay bound in the body and form the musculature and character style of a person. Energy will never rise up to the higher mind, to be expressed as thoughts, opinions, or insights. This can produce engorgement of the tissues, rigidity of the bones, and other congestive problems. The more we feel free to express ourselves, the more internal regulation we have for our mental and emotional functions. Energy wants to be free to flow in and through us.

The Throat Chakra is a spiritual center. This is where we begin to hear our inner voice and the word of God within us. This is where channeling happens. If we keep the throat closed and congested, we miss the messages given by our Higher Self. Without that awareness, we will ignore the inner voice and suppress our strength, intuition, and creativity. Without that awareness, we become susceptible to what others tell us to do and we will follow them rather than our own deep knowing.

When we listen quietly, we may hear a voice directing us to places and people who open our hearts and heal our minds. We are able to distinguish this from other voices because it comes to connect us to the world rather than isolate us; it offers solace rather than hurt or abuse. The more we are in touch with who we are, the more familiar our inner voice becomes. When we accept its guidance as reliable, we know that it comes from a place which is loving, peaceful, and good, and we can act on it in positive and conscious ways.

Well-anchored egos trust their inner knowing; they assess the attractions from the outer world and recognize their own inner voice as separate from the small child, the guilty adolescent, or the person who always must please others. There is a distinct timbre to the quality of our inner voices. It is there to bring us our highest good when we give ourselves the space to listen.

When we are negative about ourselves or life in general, we create a rent in the fine, etheric fabric of the Throat Chakra, allowing energy to leak away. What strengthens the throat is a strong will committed to life and the expression of our truth. It takes a healthy regard for the truth to stand our ground when the world is tugging at us to be someone or something other than what we are. It also takes a firm sense of personal integrity to maintain our inner sense of Self through the ups and downs of life without the need to blame others or fall into despair. Whenever we lie about others, or exaggerate, or embellish the truth we are taking energy away from the Throat Chakra. At the Throat Chakra, we need to honor our spiritual commitment, listen to our inner truth, reinforce our capacity to love, and be in our experience.

Developing a strong and resilient Throat Chakra takes time, experience, and maturity. It also takes a respect for our inner reality and a love of the higher truths, the laws by which the universe operates. Living from our truths does not come easily or quickly. It takes time to learn what is right and wholesome, what serves our highest good, and to be able to look back on the past with understanding. Accepting the purpose of all the hardships, losses, and separations we have experienced is how we develop psychologically and mature spiritually.

It can take years, maybe even a lifetime, to put the pieces of the puzzle together. If you believe in the laws of karma or have a specific philosophy about life, it will help you to create a spiritual context in which you can assess your experiences, especially the more painful and sensitive ones. By honoring our capacity to speak our truth and communicate our inner reality, we have the possibility to expand and develop our lives.

Questionnaire

The qualities of the Throat Chakra are Truth, Communication, Willpower, Creativity, and Integrity. This center encourages emotional and spiritual expression. Please look at the following questions and answer them as honestly as you can. By doing so, you open up a new channel for the truth.

Communication
• To what degree do you allow yourself to communicate your deepest feelings to others?

- Do you focus your intent on honest, open, and sincere communication?
- Do you lie to protect yourself?
- Do you lie to make yourself appear more or less important than you are?
- Do you make simple things into issues?
- Do you seek difficult or dramatic ways to enhance your self-importance?
- Do you gossip and malign others you dislike?
- Do you realize that your survival is dependent upon your ability to express yourself and communicate with others?
- Can you express your feelings with ease?
- How important is this in your communication with others?
- Do you prefer to talk about irrelevant matters in order to appear okay to others?
- Do you judge others for expressing how they feel?
- Do you place a limit on feelings you consider acceptable?
- Do you place a limit on the expression of those feelings?
- How honest are you with yourself?
- Do you feel that you can communicate with your inner Self about your deepest feelings?
- Do you become frightened when you need to speak up for yourself?
- Do you put down others who have beliefs unlike yours?
- Do you put down others whose actions are not like yours?

Integrity
- How important is your personal integrity?
- Do you do what you say you will do?
- Is there a difference between what you say you believe and how you live your life?
- Do you support those who help you?

- Do you maintain the integrity of your relationships?
- Do you speak about the things in your life that really matter to you?
- Do you feel a personal responsibility to speak about such things?
- Do you believe that you have a right to ask for the things you want?
- When you do not speak out, do you resent it when you don't get what you want?
- Can you be honest in the face of opposition even if it means disturbing others?
- Can you speak out when something is not right?
- How strongly do you value what others tell you?
- Do you get upset when others have not been straight with you or have lied to you?
- How does this affect you?
- If something terrible happened do you express your fury?
- Or do you suppress your feelings and become cynical and derogatory about the situation, or spiritual and excuse their actions, or feel your feelings and give them space to lead you to resolution?
- Can you acknowledge that the people close to you and those you work with have the right to their feelings?

Truth
- Do you honor the truths of others?
- How much importance do you give to the internal messages you receive?
- Do you listen to the truth in your body/mind/spirit?
- Do you value your inner voice sufficiently to let the truth find its way to your heart?
- How much time do you give to listening to your inner voice?
- Do you meditate on a regular basis?
- Do you tune into your inner voice through prayer, song, painting, or other creative pursuits?

- Do you keep a journal or dream diary where you can communicate your inner truth?
- Do you honor the voice within you that wants expression?
- How do you do this?
- Do you know if you channel a higher voice than your own local voice?
- Do you have a sense that the truth wants to find expression through you? This may become apparent when you are teaching or working with people on a very deep level.
- What does it want to say?

Willpower
- How strong is your will?
- Do you acknowledge that you may be overloading your will center by trying to control life?
- Are you willful in obtaining what you want in life?
- Do you push your way forward willfully to get what you want?
- Do you believe in a spiritual will that says "Not my will but Thine Be done"?
- Do you take time to listen to what that higher will is about in your life?
- Do you have the will to see things through to their proper conclusions?
- Do you have the will to hold back when it is more appropriate to be still?
- Do you have the will to incur pain and distress for what you believe in?
- Do you see that your will is part of a greater will?
- Do you do anything which diminishes your will such as substance abuse with drugs, smoking, overeating or undereating, drinking? Substance abuse is self-imposed. It is about issues of will—you do not want to know, feel, or hear your truth.
- Do you know when this is happening?
- Do you know how to arrest your impulse to sabotage your highest good?

Creativity
- How do you express your creativity?
- What gives you joy and delight in terms of personal expression?
- Do you enjoy writing, painting, dance, music?
- Do you enjoy cooking, gardening, working with wood, or fixing your car?
- Do you enjoy sports?
- What attracts you?
- Where are you creative? Creativity is a universal expression of our love for life and can be shared by people regardless of language.
- Do you see the purpose of your life to be creative?
- How can you enhance your creative expression?

Meditation

Sit with your back straight while still feeling relaxed and at ease. Tilt your nose down toward your chin and release the tension in the back of your neck. If your neck is very tight you can make head circles which will release the tension in your neck. We channel our inner truths through the back of our necks, so it is important to feel that this area of your body is soft, open, and resilient. Take a few deep breaths into your throat and sense the expansion in the back of your throat. You may feel a constriction or tightness in this area. Repeated breathing here will help loosen the tightness.

Feel your energy contained within your throat and around your mouth and ears. This is the energy of your truth, your will, and your creativity. It wants to be connected to your personal integrity through a commitment to higher spiritual values. As you release the energy of fear, swallowed anger, or pain, let go of your defiance, your pride, and your resistance. Let your jaw relax and be free. Let the control go for a few minutes.

Affirm that the truth is yours and you can always choose to express yourself in ways that support your deepest Self. Affirm your worth and the value of your communication. Know that you are always true to your inner Self, no matter what you say or do. Acknowledge that you are free to express yourself in whichever way that suits you. You can use words, creativity, or even silence to express your innermost truths.

Find delight in whichever form of expression you choose to bear your signature. At this moment assert your right to express your truth.

Throat Chakra

The Brow Chakra and Change

The Brow Chakra is one of the most important energy centers. Known as the control center, it regulates our vital functions through the hormones secreted by the pituitary gland, the ductless gland that controls our growth. Sensitive to our thoughts and emotions, it acts as a mood elevator. It assesses and evaluates our encounters and experiences as positive or negative, illuminates our experiences, and brings us inner peace and harmony when we live in correspondence with universal principles. This center has the capacity to control our responses to situations, so that we either expand in acceptance of our reality, or contract and pull away from it. Not enough can be said about the capabilities of this chakra for personal and spiritual transformation.

The Brow Chakra opens as we assume greater degrees of responsibility for ourselves and the quality of life we desire. As we grow in spirit, the mysteries of life are revealed to us so that we have the possibility of acting as co-creator with God in making our life work and helping this planet become a better place in which to live. When we choose to use this gift for the good of others and the healing of the planet, we step onto the path of our destiny.

Without change the spirit shrinks and withers. It requires that we do both internal and external work, stepping out into the unknown and going with the flow of life. Our inner growth and maturity are deeply connected with this chakra.

The Brow Chakra is where we are able to look deep within our own nature to evaluate our choices. Discernment is a quality of this center. It is where we pick and choose who and what is for our greatest good. Whenever we doubt ourselves or are in conflict with our inner knowing and outer actions, this center closes down. Our judgment becomes impaired, and we make decisions for the wrong reasons. The functioning of this center thrives on our ability to choose life-affirming situations and people who honor our nature and respond to us in wholesome, loving ways. Choosing wisely for ourselves is a result of a well-functioning Brow center.

This chakra comes into full power late in life. It takes time to have enough life experiences to garner some wisdom in order to be discerning about the path which best reflects the totality of our hopes, dreams, and desires. The center thrives when our choices reflect internalized experiences, such as wanting love, good health, security, or abundance. It works best when we seek quality and depth of experience, but it is also capable of bringing us the external things we need to survive and thrive.

It is from this center that we are able to visualize and imagine the kind of life we want. We can use this center to create our vision and then manifest the experiences that bring us what we want. It is important to decide what we want before we start to manipulate the material world. The more this center is open, the sooner we get the things we really want. That is why this center opens when we have some degree of maturity, not when we are young, foolish, or unaware of what we are doing.

This center also creates experiences of prayer, intention, and grace that teach us about the richness and beauty of life. These experiences generally reflect our attitudes and how we think about life. These experiences may not always be easy to assimilate, but they enrich our inner development and encourage us to be better people.

If we are happy and open to good things, we create more good things for ourselves. If we believe that good things are coming to us they generally do. On the other hand, if we are negative, skeptical, and frightened, these will be the types of experience we will draw to us. It is hard to convince people that they are manifesting their own reality and experiences. They prefer blaming others or giving away their power. It doesn't matter what happens—it is our attitude to what happens that determines the outcome. If we fear death and resist it, we will probably fail to experience the richness that this transition brings. There is an old expression that what you resist persists.

The Brow Chakra helps us to develop wisdom and discernment, and to use this knowledge for our highest good. It becomes activated whenever we choose to look deeply within and see the power of the mind to create. When we do this, we begin to ask what our experiences are about, evaluating them in terms of our psychic and spiritual growth. The Brow Chakra helps this growth by giving us flashes of insight and wisdom, providing us with internal awareness as we move in and out of the corridors of change. There is no point in repeating the same experiences. Once we have gained some wisdom, we move on to new levels of development and manifestation.

We deal with change from a very different point of view at this chakra. Change will not bring fear, but transformation—letting go and welcoming the new. We need this chakra to act as a beacon through the confusion. We can use our inner eye to evaluate and discern whether things are right or good for us, and help us to formulate what we want. Change brings to us new experiences, new people, and sometimes new places. Sorting them out and seeing what works for us is the function of this center.

This center starts to function along universal patterns after the Uranus Return at forty-two. This is the point in astrology where we develop more from choice than from "shoulds" or "have tos." Until that point this chakra acts as a receptor for information that we can use to find our path in work and in our daily life. Up until that point when we make positive choices for growth and maturity, most people are not resourceful enough to think for themselves. They follow trends, fashions, and the writings and thoughts of others.

Independent life choices begin to develop from age forty-two, corresponding to the Uranus return. This is the time when we have the capacity to discern and choose carefully, when we gather our forces—our gifts and ideals—to put us on the path we wish to follow. From this juncture we develop into mature adults, becoming less susceptible to the mass media, our peers, family, or church. We begin to look around and weigh our life and how we want to live it.

This transition can be very chaotic. People can die, become ill, change homes, jobs, and partners. But the promise is great: these events can shake people to the core and make them evaluate the realities of their lives. They will start to think on their own and find their own answers. They will be better able to understand the intricate workings of the human psyche and help others through change.

If people haven't shifted their thinking to a more holistic and self-accepting way by the mid-forties, their health, relationships, and what they want to do with their gifts and talents may come up for question. Their consciousness has to shift. The positive side to this transition is that out of these experiences people grow internally as they never did before. Out of life experiences, seeds begin to grow and flourish that lead to new avenues of expression, creativity, and emotional acceptance. The Brow Chakra does all it can to help the body manage changes. It stimulates the hormones that keep the body fit and prepared for change.

We have to think for ourselves in order to make appropriate choices. Sometimes we need to seek guidance and advice from those who are wiser than we are. At other times we need to step into the unknown and make our own choices. Today there are books, training programs, and courses that can help us. There are also spiritual masters and gurus who invite us to surrender our will in the interest of our highest good. We must beware of becoming automatons by letting others think for us. We then regurgitate what we have been told without thinking anything through. We lose our independence and our capacity for making optimal choices.

Good teachers, gurus, or masters should want their followers to be capable of making wise and healthy decisions for themselves, and should counsel them accordingly. Nothing then is lost in terms of self-regulation. The channels of higher consciousness are opened and the management of that new energy becomes ours to do with as we are inspired. This is how good teachers operate. They do not enslave the will of their followers, nor do they manipulate them to do their bidding.

But when a guru asks that certain practices be followed—dressing in a certain manner, chanting words, doing pujas or asanas—to link the soul of that person to the soul of the teacher, something will get lost for devotees. Their will is forfeited, their minds cease to operate, and their individuality is lost. The gurus are fed from the energy the followers project onto them. When this happens, the followers become weakened and lose their capacity to guide, inspire, or illuminate. Good teachers, on the other hand, encourage their followers to listen to their own inner knowing.

The realm of illusion, impermanence, and freedom are all related to the Brow Chakra. A chair may be an item upon which you sit. But a specific chair may represent a memory of an occasion or an exchange of ideas to you. Knowing what things are about on a meaningful level is a function of the Brow Chakra. It helps us to discern what good has come to us from certain people or places. It shows us what worked for us, and what created struggle, disharmony, and pain. It shows us the true nature of reality.

Often, when we are caught in an experience, we are unable to see its true meaning. We need a certain distance to understand its true nature. It empowers the mind to find its own way through the maze and confusion that often accompanies a difficult transformation. Basically, it requires time to reflect and transform our thinking. For instance, if we see that we have been pushing and striving for years to live creatively, or if we have been in a difficult relationship, we need to ask if it was important to be involved in this way. What did we learn from it? We may come to realize that buried within our unconscious emotional patterns is an underlying belief that nothing comes easily. Perhaps we didn't love ourselves enough. Would it not serve us to love and respect ourselves now before we get involved with another person?

Evolved people look within to find a core attitude or underlying thought. This way of thinking is inner-directed. It can be evaluated on an objective scale to reflect inner growth and healing. This way of thinking is not analytic as much as it is symbolic and imaginable. When we see a situation unfold, we should ask what it was about at a deep level that our spirit can understand. Can I accept it as I see it now? Can I let it go? Do I need to forgive? Or if I enjoyed it how do I create more of it?

These are the types of questions that a discerning mind asks in a moment of change. Sometimes there are no answers, or they will not appear until we have developed the consciousness to understand them. At other times we will find the answers thus freeing ourselves of the energy attached to the experience. We have worked it through. Answers may also appear in dreams or come to us in other unconscious ways.

Many people resist this type of thinking. Afraid they will see things that they won't like, they refuse to look within. But looking within opens the door, allowing us to perceive experiences in a true light. Some people will move from one experience to another, never reflecting, never going within, never gaining the wisdom. They will repeat the same mistakes over and over again, never understanding what happened to them. Resistance to change makes people waste their life energy, dissipate their will, and become old and exhausted before their time. They don't know how to back away from things that suck their energy. They have not developed the discrimination or the ability to know whether something is good for them or not.

The Brow Chakra provides us with the tools of wisdom, knowledge, discernment, imagination, and intuition. How we use these tools depends on how responsible we are for our own actions. We have the ability to transform ourselves at deep and wondrous levels. It is up to us.

Questionnaire

The Brow Chakra is comprised of detachment, conscious intelligence, synthetic as well as analytic thought, memory, the ability to learn (what we call education), and the ability to know what we have learned (what we call wisdom). Discernment, imagination, and intuition are also important aspects of this center. Please consider the following questions. They are part of how you imagine yourself, and how you use your intelligence.

Wisdom is also referred to as inner knowing. It relates to that part of our intelligence that knows that it knows. Wisdom is the distillation of our life experiences. Our ability to find wisdom from the events that transpired in our lives and release from the negative projections and emotions that often accompany learning are what define a mature and wise being. Most people disregard the learning or can't get past the emotions of their experiences. Unfortunately they miss the essence of life.

- How wise do you feel you are about life?
- Have you learned from your triumphs and failures in life?
- Do you respect the wisdom of others who have paid the price of their learning?
- Have you suppressed your knowing?
- What do you know about your life and the people around you?
- How do you avoid or suppress your knowing?
- How do you fail to see the signs, read the energy, or feel the feelings?
- What do you do to sabotage your knowing?
- Do you give others the power to know things for you?
- Do you invalidate your worth and your intelligence?
- Do you think you aren't smart enough to know?
- Do you give over your knowing to your family, your job, or your relationship?
- Do you give your health over to your family, job, or relationship?
- Are you willing to get back the power of your knowing?
- Are you willing to listen to your knowing when it speaks to you?
- What is your knowing about love, relationships, health, children, and your life path?
- Where is your wisdom about joy and pleasure, making and spending money, sex, or friendship?
- What do you do with your wisdom?
- Do you keep it to yourself?
- Do you share it with friends?
- Do you teach your wisdom to others?
- The Bible says that wisdom is more valuable than gold. Do you understand this?

Discernment

Discernment is defined as using your intelligence to differentiate what is good for you and what is not. It implies that you know who you are and what you want. It is the highly refined ability to sense the inner nature of things and people and to trust that your attraction or repulsion is correct.

- Do you trust your ability to know what is good for you?
- Do you know what is not good for you?
- Can you tell the difference between what feels good and what is really good for you?
- How do you know when something is good for you?
- Do you feel it inside yourself?
- Do you listen to what others tell you is good for you?
- What were you aware of when you got trapped with a person who wasn't good for you?
- What were you aware of when you were trapped in a situation that wasn't good for you?
- Were you lonely?
- Did you want to please others?
- Did you want to appear to be smart and in charge of things?
- Were you unable to say no?
- Can you define your self-sabotaging mechanism that blocks your ability to discern?
- Do you find yourself in situations that you feel you must continue and suffer with?
- Do you use your belief system to brutalize your vulnerability and fears?
- Are you aware how you punish yourself and fail to see what is good for you and what is not?

Knowledge
- How do you use knowledge to enhance your life?
- Do you believe in the importance of knowledge to help you better your life?

- Many people are now training and gathering some impressive knowledge that can be used to help people regain their sense of Self. Do you feel that you want to gather new knowledge to help improve the quality of your life?
- Does knowledge get in the way of your experience at times?
- Do you respect the power of the knowledge you are tapping into?
- Do you match these levels of knowledge with increased awareness and personal integrity?
- Do you fill your mind with information that makes you appear intelligent, but in reality blocks your depth and essence because you cannot access your emotions?
- How strongly do you rate learning?
- How much do you value external input as opposed to internal insight and experience?
- Can you visualize a balance of this in your life?
- What would it take for you to trust yourself more and rely less on external sources of learning?

Imagination

Our imagination is a gift enabling us to create reality the way we would like it to be. Many people are not encouraged to use imagination in this positive way because it is considered a waste of time.

- How do you utilize the gift?
- Do you encourage yourself to imagine what it would be like to be happy and fulfilled?
- Can you imagine how you would be under certain conditions and what your life would be like if circumstances were different?
- By not using your imagination, have you brutalized the vulnerable and sensitive child within you?

- If someone told you it is good for you to use your imagination, would this make it easier to daydream creatively and see the things you want in life?
- Imagination responds to color and sound. Do you use these tools to wake the right hemisphere of your brain to be more creative and joyful?
- Can you imagine being happy?
- Can you imagine being fulfilled?
- Can you imagine being successful?
- Can you imagine being healthy?
- Can you imagine being rested?
- Can you imagine being wealthy?
- Can you imagine being beautiful on the outside?
- Can you imagine being beautiful on the inside?
- Can you imagine being athletic?
- Can you imagine being old?
- Can you imagine being wise?
- Can you imagine being with the angels?
- Can you imagine being with the shamans?
- Can you imagine being with the fairies?
- Can you imagine being with loving friends?
- Can you imagine flying?
- Can you imagine living in (or visiting) exotic lands?
- Can you imagine living with giants?
- Can you imagine living with elves?
- Can you imagine living with mermaids?
- Can you imagine living a less ordinary life?

Intuition

Intuition is a gift of activated inner knowing. It is a way of perceiving that helps you access whether what you experience is the truth. It comes naturally to everyone, but it often ends with childhood. It is believed that twenty-five percent of all people are intuitive. Does this mean that the rest of the population is not using this gift? As with all gifts this needs to be honored and valued. It requires listening and creating a context within which you can read the signs and energy put in front of you. Trusting your intuition can be life-saving and exciting. It is a miraculous way of living your life.

- What stops you from trusting this aspect of mind?
- Are there ideas, attitudes, or programs that have made you avoid this side of your life?
- What can you do to develop your intuitive skills?
- Are you willing to access this valuable storehouse of knowing that is available to you?

Meditation

Sit comfortably and breathe deeply several times to relax your body and calm your mind. Begin to breathe and focus energy into the Brow Chakra, which sits between your eye brows. Visualize an indigo blue, large, five pointed star in this area, expanding and deepening in color. See each arm of the star representing your capacity to be wise, discerning, imaginative, intuitive, and knowledgeable. Expand that capacity with every breath. Pray for clarity, focus, and knowing in all your life experiences. Cultivate your Brow Chakra daily so that you have the presence of mind you need to stabilize during changes and transitions.

Brow Chakra

The Crown Chakra and Change

The Crown Chakra is the closest energy center to the heavens and the cosmos. It functions as an antenna, a receiver of divine energy coming to us in the form of inspiration, guidance, and protection. It is related to our experience of archetypes, guides, and angels. It opens later in life, when we have learned the spiritual nature of our existence and are able to deal with the responsibilities of serving the world and our planet. If we are prepared to develop our spirituality and accept our Divine nature, this center opens easily. It functions as a channel for the flow of cosmic energy to be used in healing, heightened consciousness, and teaching. With a vibrant, functioning Crown, we are open to the unlimited and bountiful grace of Universal Intelligence.

When this center is engaged our life becomes mystically oriented and spiritual in context. We no longer fight; we forgive. We release what clutters our path and impedes our progress toward a resilient and viable connection with God. We accept the impermanence of life and allow change to be a metaphor for growth.

The awareness that we are part of the whole and the whole is part of us is brought into living reality with the opening of the Crown Chakra. This center has been known to sages, spiritual teachers, and wise people since ancient times as the point of connection with the

Source. There are many spiritual practices to open and create a channel for the energy of Higher Powers to flow through it. When left on its own, the Crown Chakra will open when a person is ready to assimilate spiritual truths and live a life that is free of ego and receptive to the will of God. In our Western world where we generally accept the will of the ego as opposed to the will of God, we retard and stunt the opening of this center.

All great religions and spiritual cultures acknowledge the importance of this chakra. This is the place all religious devotees keep covered. Orthodox Jews, practicing Muslims, and Catholic priests cover this part of the head and acknowledge that it is sacred. Sikhs also wear turbans and grow their hair over the crown. Their traditions know that this energy center carries spiritual power.

We need a balanced energy system to make the Crown Chakra functional and healthy. If it becomes activated too soon, other parts of our energy system will not operate fully and we may experience temporary insanity, confusion, and indecision. In most spiritual practices the knowledge that opens this center is valued and guarded: it is not given to anyone who seeks enlightenment without doing the necessary rigorous work, devotion, initiations, and tests. The other way this center can open is through creativity. The Crown Chakra is also the center of inspiration, healing, beauty, and serenity. The color that governs it is violet.

It can control bodily pain and open the mind to deep contemplation of the nature of God and the workings of the cosmos. Persons on a spiritual path who are not necessarily affiliated with an official religion can open their Crown Chakra by choosing to live by their highest truths. Expressing one's inner nature in a creative way opens the Crown Chakra.

Whenever we are faced with change, this is the chakra that maintains sufficient comfort, peace, and tranquility to keep us stable. Focusing our attention in meditation helps keep this chakra active and open. It also brings us inner guidance and inspiration, and connects us to the place where our Higher Self can interface with our conscious mind.

It is often the awareness and insight that emerges from times of change that strengthens the Crown, telling us that there is another force guiding us through life. Inspiration becomes the energy and awareness that guides us along our path and delivers the ideas to us to implement. Hand in hand, wisdom and inspiration form the web that opens the door to the Infinite. With a link to the wonders and mysteries of the Universe, we accept that everything is as it should be, that we are all right and that things are being looked after from above.

People who live with the highest spiritual awareness do not often put their energies into the struggles of life. They teach, guide, and inspire others to find their own magic and cultivate their own gifts. They do their best to help others do their best to liberate themselves. Being in the presence of such enlightened people is a unique and wonderful experience. They are so light there is no effort in being with them. Their energy is fresh and free, joyful, and serenely energizing.

But most of us have different lives. As we go back into the "real world," we take part of that energy and nourish it so that it blooms into a higher spiritual awareness and maturation. As we purify our spirit through our internal efforts and external work, we divest ourselves of the heaviness and sacrifices, we transform ourselves into spiritual beings. We do not have to change the outer circumstances of our lives, only our inner attitudes. From this awareness we become one with spirit.

As we move through the uncertainties of life with this chakra open and functioning, we realize and experience the presence of divine guidance in everything we do. It inspires us as we walk our chosen path. This guidance comes in many forms. How we choose to tap into it can be whatever we need to come closer to loving and valuing ourselves. We may hear our inner voice telling us where to go or what to do. We may be shown pictures in waking or dream states that direct and guide us toward useful information. Receptivity is the intention that opens the way to manifest spirit in our lives.

The power of prayer helps us bear our burdens with grace, and whenever the going gets too rough, prayer is there. When we live in the grace of the Crown Chakra, whatever comes to us becomes an opportunity to purify ourselves. Each experience helps link us to the light of spiritual awareness and the minds of men and women everywhere.

When people live too much in the realm of spirit and when they are not grounded, this chakra can become unbalanced and symptoms that resemble madness may appear. When there is too much stimulation at this level, the whole organism may go into a form of inversion and confusion. We live in the material world and our spirit demands a strong physical body and a healthy body/mind/spirit balance. Too much connection with spirit can lead to psychic disembodiment and nervous exhaustion.

The body needs to be grounded in its material existence, the emotions anchored in consciousness and expression, and the mind opened to order and clarity so that we can handle the energy from the nonphysical world. When the energy of a higher, more refined power enters the body, it will affect the fine circuitry that feeds the nerves. People who have experienced enlightenment describe the blinding light which can accompany illumination. Whenever there is healing or channeling, the physical body uses its energy with great intensity. Disturbances can include sleeplessness, intense physical restlessness, palpitations, and loss of appetite. It is not unlike states induced by LSD or other hallucinatory drugs. When this energy enters the body the emotions can become jagged and unbalanced. Suppressed emotions will be experienced. It is such a strong surge of energy that it will force a person to be aware of lower, less enlightened realms of existence.

Taking care of the physical body, eating properly, and getting enough rest and recreation keep the body and spirit balanced.

It requires a strong will and a grounded body to manage the intensity of channeling. This is important to remember when this center starts to open and people become euphoric. Sometimes people who do this work develop serious symptoms that debilitate them. Jane Roberts who channeled SETH did not look after her health and after years of channeling suffered a slow, painful death. Some clairvoyants and psychics also develop unusual physical symptoms from their work. One minute they are fine and the next minute a surge of negative energy overwhelms them for several hours or days.

The mundane physical needs of everyday life go a long way to support a person who has a connection to the higher realms. Isolation and selective, exclusive behavior create a strong sense of separation. Sometimes, however, people living primarily in these higher realms do need solitude and privacy to soothe and protect their delicate systems.

One of the enjoyable aspects of the Crown Chakra is its affinity to beauty. Beauty opens the mind to realms of possibilities that enchant, heal, and soothe the psyche. We respond to all levels of beauty, and it provides the aesthetic basis for inspiration, desire, and appreciation. Tranquility is the space in which the illumination of beauty can take place. For instance, when we see the wonder of a Zen garden, we see simple form, balance, and harmony. The same thing happens when we see a touching verbal or nonverbal exchange between people. These are things that feed and nourish the Crown Chakra, allowing it to open with ease and grace. Where there is clutter, chaos, or disequilibrium, a sensitive person can feel acutely uncomfortable, a response from their aesthetic center in the Crown Chakra.

When we find internal harmony through acceptance or surrender to a higher power, we can create and manifest external harmony. Gardens, churches, parks, and beautiful houses are the places we can find or create the spirit of God as a living reality. Creating our own sanctuaries in our homes or in the rooms in which we live and study makes us feel that this is a space that God can enter. When our internal energy is balanced, we create an environment that is naturally rich in spirit and grace.

Serenity is a very important aspect of the Crown Chakra. It is deeper than calmness, leaving the mind peaceful—at one with itself. It puts you into the moment so that whatever you are doing is fine: there is no resistance and no separation. It does not matter where you are or what you are doing: you are in the moment and inhabiting it fully. Serenity comes when we surrender.

We can do many things to make a place feel serene. We can fill a room with flowers and plants, burn incense and candles, play quiet music, or place healing crystals around us. However, true serenity comes from accepting and being at peace with our emotions, our desires, and our very nature. It means being comfortable with who and how we are, and having the mind stilled to the point where there is no agitation, no grievance, no fear, doubt, or trauma. We are in the moment.

Serenity can be created by stepping out of time. This is an art form that puts you into the now and takes the weight of responsibility off your shoulders momentarily. Watching clouds fly over, listening to a birdsong, or hearing a beautiful piece of music make you surrender to the beauty and joy of the present. Your mind will be so engaged with the rapture of the experience that the body will have the chance to undo any stress and relax.

When people can detach and bring their minds into the moment, the brain releases endorphins that alter the biochemistry of the body. The muscles then relax and the nervous system regenerates. Learning to step out of time for a brief, unscheduled flight of freedom does much to help you realize there are other planes of existence and other ways you can respond to events.

When the Crown Chakra is activated, a deep peace descends over the body/mind/spirit. The cacophony fades away, the inner pull of the soul draws the eyes deep into the skull, and a person's consciousness becomes close to the Source. These are meditative moments full of the poignant awareness of the power of the Divine. We are all connected to the Source. It lives within each of us and has its integral identity as a living presence within us. When we live with an open Crown Chakra, this connection happens. We become one with the spirit which moves within us.

Acknowledging the Source is required when we have this level of consciousness. People who are connected to a higher power know that whatever their destiny or karma, it is part of the divine. When we connect with that place within us where that presence is living, we become one with the Source.

There is nothing that cannot be manifested or accomplished when we are connected on this level. Great masters have manifested material substance. Sai Baba, the acclaimed Indian saint, produces a substance known as Babuti, a fine dust which flows from his hands. He has been known to create gifts for his devotees out of substances from his own body. When a spirit has reached this level of conscious attainment as a human being, they must be aware of God's presence as much as possible. They can seek solitude or choose to experience other people as the vehicle through which God manifests and lives. On this level of awareness all life and everyone in it becomes a delight and joy. There is no separation, no struggle or strife. All is one and all is bliss.

Living ordinary lives precludes living in this rarefied space for more than a short period of time each day. Prayer and meditation take us to that place of connection. It is our daily reminder that life on earth is an aspect of the eternal life where the spirit is not subject to the laws of birth or death. It lives forever and its only task is to remember itself. When we live a conscious life we are spiritual. We identify with that part of ourselves where we are one with spirit, one with the soul. On this level change holds no fear. We know that life is inevitably full of change, but that it means nothing in the eternal scheme of things. All of our experiences are only part of the purification process we must undergo to be one with God. With this awareness even death holds no fear.

When we open our Crown Chakra by accepting the spiritual truths that govern the universe, we become linked eternally with the One. Our light shines and we accept the passing of time and whatever circumstances change brings to us. We lose the attachment to outcomes, we accept the inevitability of transition, and we are grateful for all the goodness that comes our way—people who have blessed our lives, places we have been privileged to visit, successes, failures, and gifts. Gratitude is the energy of an evolved person. The Crown Chakra focuses on our spiritual connection with the Infinite. It acts as a bridge between our inner sense of personal identity and our awareness of the Ultimate Source of Creation to which we are all united.

The Crown Chakra represents an enlightened state of awareness known as Samadi in Hindi. This chakra, long recognized by esoteric teachings as the thousand petal lotus, brings us into contact with the eternal, undying, and permanent part of our souls. The wisdom of each lifetime is accumulated in the center, representing total transcendence from what is fleeting, earthly, and transient. When the Crown Chakra opens, we live in the realm of spirit and align our ego with the ultimate reality. This awareness is conscious of itself and the entire universe at the same time. The significant phrase used to describe this state is: I AM THAT I AM.

Energy in this center is highly refined, light, and buoyant. It soothes and eases mental, emotional, and physical states of pain. It embraces us and cloaks us in a states of grace. We become one with all life, visible and invisible. We are connected to the Source of all creation.

Questionnaire

Beauty
- Does the love of beauty stimulate your sense of appreciation for life?
- Do you take time to see beauty in the world around you?
- Do you appreciate the wonder of music and the magic of colors?
- Is it part of your experience that music exists in your body and resonates in the higher spheres?
- Do you allow yourself to listen to your inner music, or to be soothed and touched?
- Do you allow your own beauty to shine forth or do you conform with fashion?
- How beautiful do you make your home, office, or wherever you work or meet people?
- Do you bring beauty into your life by making a lovely garden, beautiful food and meals?
- Can you see beauty in others?
- When you are around sick or dysfunctional people, can you see their inner beauty?
- Can you see the beauty in the grotesque, the weak, the aged, or the dying?

Serenity
- Have you experienced serenity?
- When does this come to you?
- When you meditate or heal do you feel serene?
- What does this feel like on a physical level?
- Can you identify it in your body?
- What does your breathing feel like when you are in this state?
- Is it light or heavy?
- What does serenity feel like emotionally?

- Do you feel love when you are feeling serene?
- What does serenity feel like on a mental level?
- What are the nature of your thoughts?
- Can you be serene and do ordinary things like shop for groceries?
- Are you willing to experience more serenity in your life?

Oneness with the Source
- What are your highest spiritual truths about yourself, life, death, change?
- Do you feel connected to the Ultimate Reality?
- What beliefs separate you from being one with the Source?
- How do you sabotage or limit the experience of this aspect of your life?
- Do you empower religion, the Church, a guru, clairvoyants, or healers to give you the answers to life?
- Are you capable of changing any negative projection that limits your sense of oneness with all life?
- Do you obsess about rituals which will invoke power to tap you into the Source?
- Do you feel that you have to do things to be loved or accepted by the Source?
- What do you empower to connect you with that which is already a part of you?
- By doing rituals, chanting, meditating, fasting, or prostrating yourself do you know the Source any better?

Meditation

As you sit quietly and reflect on your higher nature, breathe gently and easily. If there is nothing to do and nowhere to go to be at one with the Source within you, each act of being is a celebration of you and your life. This is a time to accept and love yourself totally, fully, and completely. It is a moment to give thanks for all that has been, is, and will be as a gift from the Source to you in recognition of your very being. Gently offer a word of thanks, embrace yourself, and be well within.

Crown Chakra

Conclusion

As we grow and develop, change becomes a more integral part of the way we live and do things. We have the possibility to heal ancient wounds to our spirit and to call our power back to us with each act of forgiveness and gratitude.

We are on the brink of a time of tremendous change. It will shake the earth, bringing geographical and climatic changes that will affect everyone. As this is being written, it has rained for most of the summer in Britain, heat waves are killing people in the United States, and one thousand people have lost their lives in a tidal wave in New Guinea. Fourteen million people have lost their homes in China as the Yangtse River has flooded for nearly four thousand miles. How we process these changes is important. It seems as if we are beyond control of these planetary events because they appear so enormous to our minds.

How we choose to see these catastrophes will reflect our inner state of awareness. People are making rapid changes in their lives, letting go of the old and accepting a new way of being that is much simpler, easier to manage, and not as material and acquisitive as it was in the past. As we lighten our loads externally, it is time to shift our focus on the way we see ourselves and the events that form our lives.

We have the opportunity through change to reinvent the ground rules by which we live. Our souls can become more open, more creative, more enjoyable, and more spiritual. We can take responsibility for who we are and what we want to see happen in our lives. We have the chance to accept life on better terms, as free, expressive adults who can speak their minds, defend their space, and make wise and wholesome decisions. Isn't life exciting and isn't it asking us to say YES to it?

It is time to find healing and to embrace the oneness of life. Our lives have been a series of traumas that have made us conscious of where the leaks and holes have been in our energy field. Knowledge leads us to the place where we can heal these wounds. It is no longer time to ask our friends and partners to be our healers. We need to solve our own problems by looking within and taking responsibility for repairing the damage that has occurred. In doing so, we free up the energy within us and around us. We free those upon whom we have made ourselves dependent in order to make our lives right. It is time to take the initiative and find the therapists, homeopaths, healers, and teachers who will show us how we can heal our lives. We all have this opportunity. The intelligent wayfarers will take their pain to the appropriate places so that they can develop healthy relationships not grounded in need, vulnerability, or suffering, but instead are based on love, companionship, and a sense of fun. Go lightly in the world and know that you are safe on your journey. Enjoy your changes.

First, change is part of the impermanence of life. Once we accept it we begin to free ourselves of the expectations that make us suffer. It will teach us to find the love and compassion in our hearts that we will need when change comes our way.

Secondly, and on a different level of awareness, we will need to build strong and resilient dreams that can withstand the hard knocks that inevitably come with life. If we want to manifest a dream we will need the staying power to make it happen. We need to be stable in order to bring about the kinds of changes that will make our vision turn into reality.

Thirdly, when you are recovering from a serious illness and seek help from a healer, you need to let changes happen while undergoing cure. It is a characteristic of sick people to make many changes that drain and sap their vitality. If you want to heal yourself or someone else, don't keep changing or trying new things. Allow change to happen organically, from the inside out.

Find the strength to manage change so that you are always winning no matter which way the wind blows. Knowing who you are at the core of your being will give you the resiliency to handle all changes in your life.

Godspeed and sincere good wishes for whatever life unfolds for you on your journey. You have everything you need to make your change effective and meaningful.

Ambika offers a course in LifeChanges. It runs for 18 months and examines and works with the energy of one chakra for one full weekend, every other month. The training is transformational and offers each participant a certification in Chakra Healing which qualifies them to teach and practice this particular way of bringing healing and balance. If you wish for more information you can contact Ambika at:

P.O. Box 1371

Boulder, Colorado 80306-1371

or visit her web site at:

www.ambikawauters.com

RELATED BOOKS BY THE CROSSING PRESS

Chakras and Their Archetypes: *Uniting Energy Awareness and Spiritual Growth*

By Ambika Wauters

Linking classic archetypes to the seven chakras in the human energy system can reveal unconscious ways of behaving. Wauters helps us understand where our energy is blocked, which attitudes or emotional issues are responsible, and how to then transcend our limitations.

$16.95 • Paper • ISBN 0-89594-891-5

Healing with the Energy of the Chakras

By Ambika Wauters

Chakras are swirling wheels of light and color—vortices through which energy must pass in order to nourish and maintain physical, emotional, mental and spiritual life. Wauters presents a self-help program intended to give you guidelines and a framework within which to explore and understand more about how your energetic system responds to thoughts and expression.

$14.95 • Paper • ISBN 0-89594-906-7

Homeopathic Color Remedies

By Ambika Wauters

Color has been known to have a strong influence on people and treatment with colored light has been used in naturopathic circles for several decades. Wauters' homeopathic color remedies serve as medicine for our energy body, increasing the energetic flow physically, emotionally, and mentally.

$12.95 • Paper • ISBN 0-89594-997-0

Channeling for Everyone: *A Safe Step-by-Step Guide to Developing Your Intuition and Psychic Awareness*

By Tony Neate

This is a clear, concise guide to developing our subtler levels of consciousness. It provides us with safe, step-by-step exercises to prepare for and begin to practice channeling, allowing wider states of consciousness to become part of our everyday lives.

$12.95 • Paper • ISBN 0-89594-922-9

Clear Mind, Open Heart: *Healing Yourself, Your Relationships and the Planet*

By Eddie and Debbie Shapiro

The Shapiros offer an uplifting, inspiring, and deeply sensitive approach to healing through spiritual awareness.

$16.95 • Paper • ISBN 0-89594-917-2

RELATED BOOKS BY THE CROSSING PRESS

Color and Crystals: *A Journey Through the Chakras*
By Joy Gardner-Gordon

Information about color, crystals, tones, personality types, and Tarot archetypes that correspond to each chakra. Fully illustrated, indexed and well-organized.

$14.95 • Paper • ISBN 0-89594-258-5

Crystal Enchantments: *A Complete Guide to Stones and Their Magical Properties*
By D. J. Conway

D. J. Conway's book will help guide you in your choice of stones from Adularia to Zircon, by listing their physical properties and magical uses.

$16.95 • Paper • ISBN 1-58091-010-6

Essential Reiki: *A Complete Guide to an Ancient Healing Art*
By Diane Stein

This bestseller includes the history of Reiki, hand positions, giving treatments, and the initiations. While no book can replace directly received attunements, Essential Reiki provides everything else that the practitioner and teacher of this system needs, including all three degrees of Reiki, most of it in print for the first time.

$18.95 • Paper • ISBN 0-89594-736-6

The Healing Energy of Your Hands
By Michael Bradford

Bradford offers techniques so simple that anyone can work with healing energy quickly and easily.

$12.95 • Paper • ISBN 0-89594-781-1

Pocket Guide to Chakras
By Joy Gardner-Gordon

This book will answer your questions about chakra, including explaining what they are, where they are, how they function and what causes the chakras to open and close.

$6.95 • Paper • ISBN 0-89594-949-0

The Sevenfold Journey: *Reclaiming Mind, Body & Spirit Through the Chakras*
By Anodea Judith & Selene Vega

Combining yoga, movement, psychotherapy, and ritual, the authors weave ancient and modern wisdom into a powerful tapestry of techniques for personal growth and healing.

$18.95 • Paper • ISBN 0-89594-574-6

RELATED BOOKS BY THE CROSSING PRESS

Shamanism as a Spiritual Practice for Daily Life

By Tom Cowan

This inspirational book blends elements of shamanism with inherited traditions and contemporary religious commitments. An inspiring spiritual call.—Booklist

$16.95 • Paper • ISBN 0-89594-838-9

We are the Angels: *Healing Your Past, Present, and Future with the Lords of Karma*

By Diane Stein

Stein masterfully presents a detailed understanding of karma and the process of healing karmic patterns. She introduces the Lords of Karma, the supreme karmic record keepers able to grant requests for changed or released karma to those who ask for it.

$16.95 • Paper • ISBN 0-89594-878-8

Wind and Water: *Your Personal Feng Shui Journey*

By Carol J. Hyder

This book presents Feng Shui as simple suggestions that can be done on a daily basis-each page will provide information and a corresponding activity. Instead of reading about Feng Shui, this book will provide an immediate experience of Feng Shui.

$19.95 • Paper • ISBN 1-58091-050-5

Wisdom of the Elements: *The Sacred Wheel of Earth, Air, Fire, and Water*

By Margie McArthur

Drawing on her knowledge of neo-pagan tradition, as well as Traditional Chinese Medicine, energy work with the chakras, and Native American wisdom, McArthur gives us keys to the intricate correspondences between the Elements, the planet and our psychic landscape.

$16.95 • Paper • ISBN 0-89594-936-9

To receive a current catalog from The Crossing Press
please call toll-free, 800-777-1048.
www.crossingpress.com